AF267426

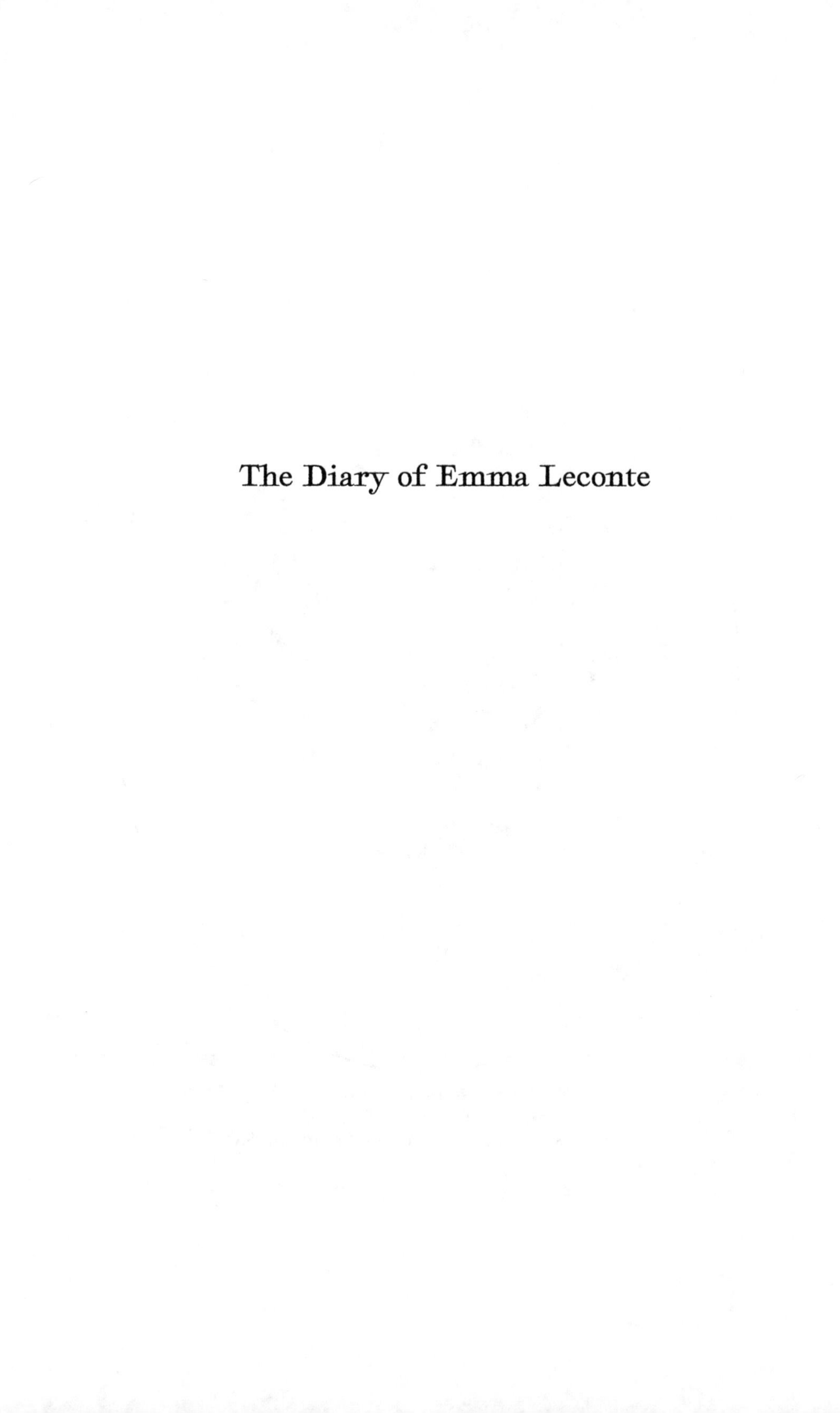

The Diary of Emma Leconte

Emma Florence LeConte.
South Caroliniana Library,
University of South Carolina, Columbia, S.C.

The Diary of
Emma LeConte

A Story of War & Survival
1864–1865

Edited by
James E. Kibler, Jr., and Karen Stokes

Introduction by
James E. Kibler, Jr.

Textual Introduction by
Karen Stokes

Green Altar Books
Shotwell Publishing

Published by
Green Altar Books, an imprint of
SHOTWELL PUBLISHING LLC
Post Office Box 2592
Columbia, So. Carolina 29202
www.ShotwellPublishing.com

Cover Image: Emma Florence LeConte portrait and "View of Sidney Park from the John Taylor House" by Augustus Grinevald, ca. 1859. Courtesy of the South Caroliniana Library, University of South Carolina, Columbia, S.C.

Cover Design: Sylvia Shealy Creations

ISBN: 978-1-963506-54-9

FIRST EDITION
10 9 8 7 6 5 4 3 2 1

PRODUCED IN THE REPUBLIC OF SOUTH CAROLINA

Contents

Introduction

James E. Kibler, Jr.

The diary of young Emma Florence LeConte is one of the most graphic primary documents of civilian experience in the war that raged in America from 1861 to 1865. Born on 10 December 1847, Emma was only seventeen when she and her family experienced the occupation, plunder and burning of Columbia, South Carolina, in February 1865. When she wrote her diary, she lived on the campus of South Carolina College, where her father Joseph was a professor.

Joseph Quarterman LeConte was born in Liberty County, Georgia, in 1823. In 1850, fifteen years before Emma penned her work, Joseph, his wife Bessie (Caroline Elizabeth Nisbet), and their two and a half year-old daughter Emma had moved to a house on the campus of Harvard University, where he went to study with the celebrated Swiss-born naturalist, Professor Louis Agassiz (1817-1873). During his sojourn in the North, LeConte made what he called "life-long friends" of Agassiz, the Yale geologist and mineralogist James Dwight Dana (1813-1895), mathematician and astronomer Professor Benjamin Peirce (1809-1880), geologist Arnold Guyot, physicist Joseph Henry, geologist and paleontologist James Hall (1811-1898), physicist Alexander Dallas Bache of the United States Coast Survey (1806-1867), and geologists William and Henry Rogers. As he said in his autobiography, he had "daily contact on the most intimate terms" with botanist Asa Gray (from whom he took a course in botany), and poets Longfellow, Lowell, and Holmes. He said he met author Richard Dana "thrice every day" and saw Ralph Waldo Emerson occasionally. Bessie, he added, "associated intimately with the families of the professors," especially with those of Agassiz, Peirce, and Cornelius Felton, the classical scholar. Boston, he said, offered the "greatest musicians." In November 1850, Emma's sister, Sarah Elizabeth ("Sallie"), the LeContes' second child, was born in Cambridge. Accordingly, the family called her "the Little Yankee."

From 1853 to January 1857, the family lived in Athens, Georgia, while Joseph was professor of geology, botany, and natural theology at Franklin College, his alma mater from which he and his brother John graduated in 1841. Emma was six when she went to Athens. In January 1857, when she was nine, the family moved to Columbia, where Joseph taught chemistry and geology at the college.

Emma's Uncle John LeConte and his wife Eleanor Josephine Graham LeConte (Emma's "Aunt Josie") had preceded them to Columbia. Uncle John was professor of physics at the college. Joseph's biographer, Lester D. Stephens, wrote that the LeContes' move to South Carolina College "helped to push that institution to the forefront of science in the antebellum Deep South" (*Joseph LeConte* [Baton Rouge: L.S.U. Press, 1982], 51). The college, with its scholars, unsurpassed library collection, and new library building, the first such separate library building in any American college, actually rivaled the best institutions nationally and not just the South.

As at Harvard, so at South Carolina College, Emma and her family lived on campus. This was Emma's home from the age of nine to twenty-one. When her parents moved to the College of California in August 1869, where Joseph became professor of geology, Emma remained in the South as the new wife of Farish Carter Furman. They were married in March 1869. Furman, grandson of the Charleston theologian, essayist, and poet the Reverend Richard Furman, was one of Joseph's former pupils. Joseph called his future son-in-law "fine, energetic, and talented." Emma and her father were close, and Joseph wrote in his autobiography that it was "a bitter trial for us to leave her and place a whole continent between us." He related that Emma "was one of the strongest and yet the gentlest, most refined and most beautiful characters I ever knew." "It may sound strange," he added, but "I not only love but actually reverence my own child" (Stephens, 109-110).

Joseph LeConte did not want to leave Columbia, but because he had worked for the Confederacy, the doors of institutions during Reconstruction were closed to him. Emma's sister Carrie recalled in her reminiscences that mother "was wont to say that my father could not have gotten a position in a primary school" (*'Ware Sherman*, xvii). The "trial" of leaving the ruined South, though "bitter," was encouraged by his scientist friends at Harvard and Yale. Agassiz, Peirce, Dr. John Torrey, and Professor Ben Silliman all wrote letters and used their influence to get LeConte the professorship in California. His friends declared that if he remained in Columbia, the new regime during Reconstruction would change the place so fundamentally as to make him feel a foreigner in his own land.

Of the Columbia years, Joseph declared in his autobiography in 1901, "My life in Columbia was perhaps the most pleasant in my whole career. The society was the most refined and cultivated I have ever known. My wife was delighted." This "most pleasant" and "most refined and cultivated" life in Columbia included the society experienced at Harvard, Athens, and Berkeley. Interestingly, Lester Stephens' biography of Joseph fails to note this important assessment.

Columbia's beauty was extolled in many sources in the decades before the war. Yet another such description has just surfaced. Prominent New York City merchant George Baxter in a letter to his wife on 11 March 1854, wrote of Columbia: "We are more & more pleased with this place. It is well termed the garden of the South. Every house has its garden & shrubbery, & the houses, cottage style, are all in good order." Baxter corroborated Joseph's comments on Columbia society. Of the Hamptons, Baxter wrote without understanding the importance of the philosophical underpinnings of the Southern gentry: "They eschew all society but the Planters—as [if] the growing of cotton was any better than selling it." Here is yet another instance of the cultural divide between the two regions on the eve of the war. (Hampton Family Papers, 1831-1932, newly archived, South Caroliniana Library.)

LeConte continued that the city's several institutions of learning "formed the nucleus about which gathered many intellectual men and women." In 1865, the men outside his circle of college faculty included paleontologist, author, and art collector Dr. Robert W. Gibbes, poet Henry Timrod, theologian James Henley Thornwell, and novelist and poet William Gilmore Simms. Dr. Gibbes was particularly noteworthy. Gibbes published his volume *The Present Earth: The Remains of a Former World* in 1849, a decade before Charles Darwin, and a year before LeConte went to Harvard to study with Agassiz. Based on his research upon fossilized shark's teeth and extinct marine mammals, Gibbes concluded that the earth was millions of years older than considered, and reconciled his belief with Scripture. Although not mentioned in studies of LeConte, Gibbes' influence was no doubt powerful, especially in reconciling science and religion, a topic for which LeConte is known today. The women in Columbia in 1865 included poet, dramatist, and essayist Louisa Cheves McCord, poet and biographer Mrs. Elizabeth F. Ellet, and diarist Mary Boykin Chesnut. In Columbia, Joseph recalled in his autobiography that "my intellectual activity was powerfully stimulated, and I wrote many articles, mostly of a literary and philosophical nature."

Of the students at the college, LeConte said they were perhaps a little too spirited at times, but they had the highest sense of honor, of right and wrong, and the deepest scorn of lies and dishonesty he had ever witnessed, before or since. He wrote that upon leaving Columbia for California, his students presented him "a splendid Bible—a really magnificent one...as an expression of appreciation for my Sunday lectures...the only present that I would have accepted" (*'Ware Sherman*, xxiv). He later shaped these Sunday lectures in Columbia into his first published book *Religion and Science* (New York: Appleton, 1873). Emma, now married and living in Georgia, longed to see her father a continent away. According to Stephens, her "longing for a return to the place of her youth led her to take a trip to Columbia in the summer of 1870. She sent ivy leaves from the old home to her parents, and they wept" (*Joseph LeConte*, 117). Joseph responded to Emma in a letter of 7 June 1870: "I can hardly think of any place as home to you & myself except Columbia and the old ivy-covered house in the campus" (as quoted in Stephens, 117).

In her unpublished memoir written in 1931, Emma left a detailed description of their campus home. The setting in which her diary was composed was a solid three-storey red-brick structure built in 1836 as the "Third Professor's House," today called "Lieber College." It had a two-storey piazza at the rear which ran the length of the building. Emma had the north-facing second-storey bedroom with a view of the college library directly across the campus lawn. Emma wrote that her two bedroom windows, framed deeply in ivy, "looked out upon the beautiful campus with its oaks and spreading elms, through which gleamed the great white columns of the library opposite" (Memoir, 33). The Eugene D'Ovilliers painting of the campus done around 1850 shows the ivy Emma describes as beginning to grow profusely around her windows on the western (right) side of the building's north (front) façade.

The large "Third Professor's House" at the time the LeContes lived there was divided down the middle as a duplex. The eastern half was the home of the family of Professor John Lawrence Reynolds, the eminent classicist. Emma often affectionately mentioned "the boy next door," Lawrence Jr., in both her diary and memoir. Emma's father had classes on the ground floor of the house. As Emma's memoir noted, this arrangement often required the inconvenience of moving books back and forth from the family's second-floor library to the downstairs classrooms.

Emma's memoir gave a detailed description of her bedroom. It was wall-papered in a patterned blue and white. A glass-doored cabinet had "shelves of minerals, agates, crystals, shells, etc." An étagère held her books. Her furniture was oak. The big fireplace had a high mantel. Her bedroom walls had steel engravings and a coloured lithograph of the *Madonna della Ledia*. She recalled that "I sat to read and study" near the front windows in "a little wicker rocking chair by the dressing table" (Memoir, 35). This is where she likely wrote her diary.

Her bedroom shared the second floor with her young sister's smaller room, a broad hallway, a parlour, and the family library. The library was "in the back and opened by long windows on the back piazza." There were "folding doors between the rooms." Two sides of the library "were lined with tall book shelves" and it had other book shelves by the fire place. Between the windows sat her father's "tall writing desk." A large library table sat "in the centre with a drop light, around which we gathered in the evening for reading aloud—Walter Scott or Shakespeare, or some such....Fine line engravings...were scattered all over the house."

Emma recalled that during the war, "many of my hours were spent in the dear familiar library....I could read to my heart's content or practise my music." She reflected in 1931 that this family library "has always been to me the ideal of a livable room. It is very dear to me in memory as it was in fact at the time....I cared too little for young companions and never seemed to miss them with the books at home and the great college library across the campus" (Memoir, 17-19). The college library was "great" indeed during her residence there, for it had the largest non-theological holdings of any American college in its day and was housed in its splendid new building (Daniel W. Hollis, *University of South Carolina*, I [1951], 136 and James E. Kibler, *The Classical Origins of Southern Literature*, 22-24).

Emma's youngest sister Carrie also left a description of the LeContes' campus home in her reminiscence. She wrote, "As a child between two and five, my playthings and picture books were illustrated tomes on archeology and engraved plates of the works of Hesiod, Aeschylus, Sophocles, Shakespeare, Goethe, and so forth." She recollected that her doll was a human skeleton in the college museum, "beautiful beyond comparison and worthy of all affection" (*'Ware Sherman*, xvi).

In 1860 the college built the "Fourth Professor's House" for Emma's Uncle John and Aunt Josie LeConte and their three children, Lula, Jules, and Johnnie. It sat at the southeast corner of Pendleton and Sumter streets, a few hundred yards north of Emma's home. This large detached two-storey brick house had a wide front piazza in the current popular Italianate style, designed by the most prominent Columbia architect, George Edward Walker.

Joseph LeConte noted that during the pillage and burning of Columbia, "several attempts to set my brother's house a-fire were thwarted by constant watchfulness" and thus escaped the conflagration (*'Ware Sherman*, 142). In order to make room for the new war memorial building, the home was moved to the rear of the library and restored in 1934. It sits there today as "Flinn Hall." Emma spent many happy hours there.

She and her Aunt Josie were close. Emma said that she was her aunt's "pet" and Jules and Johnnie were more like brothers than cousins because while in Columbia, she had no real brothers. She grew to think of Lula as another sister. In both her diary and memoir, Emma noted that when she walked to and from town, she would often see her Aunt Josie and the cousins sitting on the piazza and would speak from the street or sometimes stop in for a visit to share the news of the day.

Emma's favorite Aunt Josie was acclaimed a beauty. In his autobiography Joseph called her "the most beautiful woman I have ever seen." At Yale and Harvard Benjamin Peirce and his coterie regarded her as "The Queen" for her charm and beauty (Edward Hogan, *Of the Human Heart: A Biography of Benjamin Peirce*, 144-147). She was also noted for her convivial and happy nature. Beginning in 1861 she served as a volunteer at the Ladies' Hospital and later the Confederate hospital on the college campus. There she worked with Louisa McCord. A fellow worker remembered Josie as "the soul of fun, and gave us many a hearty laugh" (Mrs. J. P. Adams, in Smythe, *South Carolina Women in the Confederacy*, 81). She was apparently a contrast to Emma's mother, who was rather more serious. It appears from her diary and memoir that Emma, although devoted to both her parents, was closer to her father.

Beginning in October 1860, and during the first years of the war, Emma attended the Columbia Female Academy in its large and elegant Italianate building designed by architect George Edward Walker and newly constructed on Plain (now Hampton) Street in 1859. There she had French lessons in grammar and reading from Eugene D'Ovilliers, whom Emma described as "a very polished elderly Frenchman" and a talented painter. D'Ovilliers was born in Paris in 1818. Emma also had classes from "the Misses Reynolds—two maiden ladies—the elder a small, dried up, decidedly little lady—the younger her niece, gentler but very pious. Miss Jane taught English history, etc. Miss Sophia the sciences" (Memoir, 1).

Young Emma also benefited greatly from her father's position at the college and was an integral part of his and her mother's society on campus. Emma said that her father took her out of the Academy in 1863 and taught her himself. There were daily lessons variously in Latin (Virgil), Science, and Math with "systematic reading in history, philosophy, etc.," followed by "several hours of practise on the piano." She also had access to her father's campus chemistry lab (Memoir, 32, 55).

By 1865, when she began her diary at the age of seventeen, she had completed her father's instruction in both chemistry (from the textbook he used in his college classes) and plane, solid, and conic geometry (Memoir, 31). He also led her on botanical field trips in the woods and fields around the town. Emma wrote, "Father was teaching me Botany in Spring 1865 and I became familiar with the flora all around Columbia" (Memoir, 47). This and earlier field trips around Macon, Georgia, in the early 1850s were Joseph's introductions to the exploration of the natural world that would lead several decades later to the founding of the Sierra Club and a close association with the naturalist John Muir.

Emma stated of her father, "It is well-known what an interesting lecturer he was and the more so that he had the use of his laboratory at the College for my benefit" (Memoir, 32). She added that he often "had leisure to give such long talks beyond the recitation time—was ever a child so blessed—what ought I not to have been with such an influence. And the books and works of art surrounding my childhood! Father guiding my reading, forming tastes and opinions—How little we realise what we simply take for granted." In the summer of 1863, "I read much history" and "had become so expert at knitting that I could knit and read at the same time—This summer it was not only socks for the soldiers, but I had to knit stockings for myself. I knit several pair while reading Gibbon's *Decline and Fall*!" She added, "And I had learned to sew too, and learned to make my own clothes. Yellow homespun underclothing. We were weaving homespun for dresses too this winter—the mills were producing neat plaids and stripes" (Memoir, 35-36).

By 1863, Emma noted in her memoir, "I had a very good reading knowledge of French, and Mr. D'Ovilliers had turned me over to his mother, the Madame, a dear little old French woman who could scarcely speak any English at all. From her I took conversation lessons for several years and I became very fond of her. She was very polite with our mistakes—much more than we with hers when she tried to speak English" (Memoir, 53). Madame D'Ovilliers was Minde Zoe D'Ovilliers (1847-1888), the widow of Michel D'Ovilliers, formerly an engineer at the court of Napoleon Bonaparte, who left France with his wife and sons after the fall of the empire. The D'Ovilliers family lived in a large cottage on Plain (now Hampton) Street near the Female Academy, seven blocks northeast of Emma's home "and thither I walked two or three times a week, to my lessons—three or four of us—we made a pleasant circle" (Memoir, 26).

During this time, she also had piano lessons from a young prodigy, eighteen year-old Joe Denck, Jr., who, as Emma recalled, ended his life tragically by suicide (Memoir, 27). At age thirteen in 1860, young Denck had already toured Europe to great acclaim. He played violin as well as piano and accompanied his father who played flute. Joseph Denck, Sr., a German gentleman who taught music in Charleston before moving to Columbia, was married to Charlotte Hart, also said to be "possessed of rare musical abilities" and with "a passionate fondness for music." Before her marriage in around 1846, Charlotte was "a leader in the fashionable circles of Columbia" during the decade of the 1840s (Simms, *Letters,* IV, 309-310.) Emma's father also played the flute. This was the musical circle to which Emma had access. Despite the war, she tried to remain devoted to her piano practice.

Emma's diary and memoir reveal that in the last year of the war, from January to August 1865, she was keeping up with her language studies. She had mastered both French grammar and conversation sufficiently to give lessons to a lady (the diary's Mrs. Clara Blight Leland) in exchange for instruction in German. Mrs. Leland, born in Edinburgh, had been a governess in Germany and spoke the language fluently. Emma's diary for 1 April stated: "I have long wanted to get a reading knowledge of this language and have eyed wistfully the sealed treasures of German literature in the library." She learned German well enough to translate Goethe, and Schiller's drama *Wilhelm Tell*, certainly no easy accomplishment. In June 1865, she was translating twelve to fourteen pages of German a day. She related that at Mrs. Leland's, "We read German classics—prose and poetry" (Memoir, 74). Her facility in language was apparently exceptional, for *Wilhelm Tell* is not an easy work to translate, as I can myself attest, because I also did so in an undergraduate German class devoted to translating five Schiller plays under the tutelage of Professor Kyle Leighton-Faxford de Gravelines on the same University of South Carolina campus a short distance from the LeConte home, exactly a century later in 1965.

During the eight months of 1865, a time span that included the burning of Columbia in February, Emma read Madame de Stael's *De la Littérature* and Jules Michelet's *Histoire de France*, translated some of Lady Mary Wortley Montague's *Letters and Works* from English into French, and found Madame D'Ovilliers' favourite Voltaire's epic poem

L'Henriade "very dull" (Memoir, 53). Emma also took part in an encore performance of a French comedy *L'Enfant Gaté,* written and directed by Madame D'Ovilliers.

In mid-1865, Emma continued her study of history begun under the instruction of her father by rereading Gibbon. She read Thomas Carlyle's *Essays,* some of the Koran, and a biography of Mohammed. She read a novel by Charles Dickens and reread one by Sir Walter Scott. She noted that in studying paleontologist-geologist Edward Hitchcock's *The Religion of Geology and Its Connected Sciences* (1851), she lamented not having her father to help her with the "metaphysical portion" (Diary, 8 March 1865). Like Dr. Robert W. Gibbes, Hitchcock was another early disciple of the theory that the earth was millions of years old. He sought to reconcile the "old earth" geological record with the Bible by advocating what he called "gap creationism" to explain the earth's antiquity.

That Joseph knew this work and assigned it to Emma is significant, although not mentioned in either Stephens' biography of LeConte or his *Science, Race, and Religion in the American South.* While in Columbia, Joseph in fact gave the aforementioned series of Sunday lectures which became his first published book, *Religion and Science,* in 1873. As Emma envisioned the possible destruction of her father's library as the city was in flames, she wrote in a discarded page of her diary, "I thought of father's library, every book of which I love—I thought of my own dear room—Oh it was dreadful."

An indication of her father's similar love of books, and especially literature, appears in his journal account of his adventures in hiding out from Sherman's army in February 1865. Joseph said he was reading a novel by G. P. R. James while he was hiding in the bushes and the Yankees were swarming in the fields around him. The soldiers "were popping at everything they could see," but "I became so deeply absorbed in one of James's novels that I forgot entirely the presence of the Yankees" save when they came exceptionally near ('*Ware Sherman,* 42). In his strange dance of evasion, he imagined he was "like the benighted Athenian chasing the voice of Puck through the woods in *Midsummer Night's Dream*" (127). Joseph recounted that he and his companion Capt. Green "relieved the tedium [of hiding] by discussing Poetry, the

Drama, Science and Philosophy" ('*Ware Sherman*, 133). A California friend said that late in life Joseph "quoted poetry by the volume, and seemed to have an unlimited store in his memory"—especially the "beautifully descriptive and the humorous" (Stephens, 256). One of the humorous poems was no doubt Samuel Butler's *Hudibras*, a satire on the Puritan which he quoted in '*Ware Sherman* (114).

In her diary entry for 27 June 1865, four months after Columbia was burned, Emma wrote that she was once again beginning to find her books "a blessed resource—to be able to lose myself in their world and forget the world of trouble around me." Both father and daughter valued books on wide-ranging subjects, and it is natural that they would both become writers. Emma, her sister Carrie, and Joseph were all writers of clear, forceful, and engaging prose. In 1865, Emma also had the duty of teaching her younger sisters Carrie and Sallie. Carrie's "An Introductory Reminiscence" to her father's '*Ware Sherman* is ample proof of her literary talent. Emma's diary, in fact, states that she might try to become a teacher in order to make a living or to add to the family's meagre income. She would no doubt have made a most capable one.

Carrie wrote that in February 1865 "our family were saved from starvation by our negroes, who foraged about for food. Nobody asked where it had come from—either begged or stolen" ('*Ware Sherman*, xv). Emma's diary and Joseph's autobiography attest to the help that Joseph's man-servant Henry LeConte gave to the family in their time of trial. Emma wrote that Henry "hid in his room" to escape soldiers who were seeking to force him to leave with them. Emma's mother protected him from one particular soldier, whom Emma described as "the dirtiest, meanest looking creature imaginable." Henry, she continued, "vows he will never leave us unless dragged away" (Diary, 18, 19 February). Henry's wife, Mary Ann, the LeContes' cook and primary house servant, was "distressed at the thought of leaving the master and mistress who had supplied the place of father and mother to her, an orphan" (Diary, 19 February). Mary Ann said, however, that she would go with her husband if he was forced to leave. Luckily, she did not have to, for Henry evaded conscription.

The LeConte house was backed by a moderately-sized pasture, so the family, including Henry, began a vegetable garden and acquired two cows that Mrs. LeConte named Hook and Crook. Carrie noted that her mother sold their extra milk to the occupation garrison, and the family, as Mrs. LeConte put it humorously, "lived by Hook and Crook" ('*Ware Sherman*, xvi).

Joseph's autobiography noted that after the burning of Columbia, he had difficulty giving his daughters the pleasures of a social life in the burned city. He wrote that poverty and hardship, however, did not prevent diversion, for "as everybody was poor the gatherings were almost totally without expense, and therefore frequent; the hostess simply furnished lemonade and cake and the young men a negro fiddler," to whom they each paid fifty cents. Carrie added, "That was the time when the ladies danced in calico or cheap tarletan and the refreshments at an evening party consisted of a bucket of ice water" ('*Ware Sherman*, xvi-xvii).

Emma elaborated in her memoir: "The girls furnished the house—there were no refreshments. The boys furnished the music. Jim Mayrant and two other darkies—two fiddlers and a bass viol. Jim called the figures and was very enthusiastic, especially when the attendance was good." Jim would look over the crowd and assess the number of men, for each was to contribute 50 cents for his pay. The dances were quadrilles, lancers, waltzes, square dances, gallops, and *deux temps*. Emma recorded, "There was little thought given to dress—we were all on a dead level of poverty." The only party dress she had was the white muslin she had worn as a bridesmaid to the wedding of Mary Palmer described in her memoir (86-87). Joseph added, "My daughters were in their teens and for their sakes we entered heartily into the general gaiety."

Emma corroborated her father's account of his dismay at getting her out of the library, but added, "Father, distressed that my young life, embittered by the gloom of a dreadful war, should have had no natural outlet, tried so hard to help me....Poor father, to induce me to go out—in the absence of escorts—would take me himself and come for me at midnight. All the central part of town was in ruins and vehicles unknown—this often meant a walk of a mile or more." After several months of this encouragement, and no longer a shy "frequent wall flower" who had to "rack my brain for 'something to say,'" Emma added that Father "was soon concerned by the opposite score!" (Memoir, 67-68).

Apparently Emma's reputation for "learning and intellectuality" at first intimidated would-be boyfriends (69). A year later, she would describe her changed social status as "my frivolous days" (68). She became very popular and had many beaux. Her primary ornament was "my long and abundant hair" that she wore in carefully plaited braids (78). It was at this time that she met her future husband, a former cadet at the Citadel before going to war, and afterwards a student at South Carolina College, where Joseph taught him and from which he graduated.

In Carrie's first Christmas in California, the six-year-old recalled that there was a "huge box of toys," and she asked her parents, "Why didn't Santa Claus come to the little boys and girls of Columbia?" She remembered looking up from the bounty of playthings and wondering why "my father's and mother's eyes were filled with tears" (*'Ware Sherman*, xviii). The family, now separated from Emma at Christmas for the first time, no doubt also had her in mind.

Emma recalled that at the time she kept her diary she was "naturally reticent" in most matters, and that included religion. She did not favour the Presbyterian denomination, although she and her family attended Columbia's First Presbyterian Church (Memoir, 65). Emma further reported that her parents took no "active part in the work or interests of the congregation, and as I grew up all my social relations were with Trinity [Episcopal Church]" which was located on Sumter Street less than three blocks from the LeConte home. She recorded that First Presbyterian's pastor, Dr. Benjamin Palmer, asked her father to be an elder, but Joseph "told him he was not sufficiently orthodox for that office." Emma added, "Not only Father's ideas on Evolution, but on other Calvinistic doctrines were far from agreeing with the true blue Presbyterian stripe." She concluded, "Beyond going to church regularly on Sunday morning, I could not be said to have been brought up a Presbyterian" (Memoir, 43). For one thing, it is clear that unlike the "blue Presbyterians," she learned to like dancing too much and helped form a dance club in the city after the war. Emma makes it pointedly clear that even though she was moved by the Reverend Dr. Palmer's "flowing" eloquence, the Presbyterian Church "could never have satisfied my spiritual nature" (Memoir, 65).

Emma's diary, as she said in her memoir, "was written on quires of brownish Confederate letter paper" (61). On another "quire of dingy Confederate paper," and near the D'Ovilliers' cottage on Plain (Hampton) Street, another diarist was also recording the stirring events of the day. From 20 July 1864 to 11 February 1865, Mary Boykin Chesnut left the manuscript of her now famous work open on her desk in her parlour, and Confederate officers spread their maps on it to plan strategy. Neither knew that they, who were to become two of the war's most significant diarists, were working only blocks away from each other in the same attempt to capture the times. Emma must have passed Mrs. Chesnut's home many times on the way to classes at the nearby Female Academy.

Emma took her diary with her when she married in March 1869 and "finding it was wearing to pieces," and its pencil was "fading into illegibility—I undertook to copy it—or at least most of it—what seemed of any general interest." With her usual modesty, she added, "Father's of course is more worthwhile—but with its description of the destruction of Columbia even a girl's account may be of some value in supplementing his story" (Memoir, 61). In her insistence on downplaying her importance, and in avoiding calling attention to herself, she exhibited the aristocratic high culture of her upbringing.

Like a character in a Jane Austen novel, Emma often commented in her memoir on the susceptibility of her younger sisters, cousins, and girlfriends to a handsome face and the often tearful results of infatuation. She rarely records an outward display of her own emotion, although it is clear from her diary that she felt deeply and passionately. One notable exception of unrestrained grief was the touching description of her reaction to the news of the death of General Stonewall Jackson, an emotion of which she was obviously not ashamed. She wrote, "I will never forget the grief of that 10th of May [1863] with its tragic news....I shut myself in the parlour and wept as if my heart would break" (Memoir, 31). The heart broke in private, it should be noted.

Emma's diary provides a detailed first-hand look at the way of life in the household of one of America's great scientists. Joseph LeConte's contributions have been treated elsewhere, most notably in Lester Stephens' *Joseph LeConte*. The LeConte family back to the early 1700's, as Carrie noted in her introduction to *'Ware Sherman*, were "men of science from father to son" in the forefront of American intellectual endeavor (xxv). Most recently, Edward Hogan in his biography of Benjamin Peirce, has concluded of the unbroken line of scientist LeContes, "Probably no other family of the time contributed as much to American science" (145). It was their tradition. Emma's diary shows the everyday workings of the LeConte intellect in upholding that tradition. Her diary and memoir prove that Emma herself exhibited that intellect in no small measure.

Her writing also portrays a key strength of the LeConte family in providing the stability needed to maintain and further that tradition. Family solidarity and the closely interwoven lives of its members were powerful stays against the tremendous chaos of the times. Emma mentions at least twelve cousins, seven aunts, and four uncles on a regular basis in the period of her diary's eight months. Many more appear in her memoir. Emma knew them well. As we have seen, of several of the male cousins, like Jules and Johnny LeConte, for example, Emma remarked that they were really more like brothers.

The complicated knit of family portrayed in Emma's diary, common in the South of old, is portrayed here once again. The diary is yet another proof that describing the South as one vast cousinage is not too great an exaggeration. The diary shows the ways that family solidarity and interconnectedness helped Emma survive the trauma of horrific invasion and its devastating aftermath. Through all their travails, she and the other LeContes carried on with dignity and never resorted to self-pity. Emma's moving diary once again testifies to the truism that surviving rather than flourishing has always been a Southern specialty.

Ballylee
Oct. 2020-Sept. 2021

Textual Introduction

Karen Stokes

This edition is the first to present the diary just as Emma left it, or as closely as possible, and without modernization of spelling, capitalization, and punctuation. Emma's dashes in her handwritten 1870s copy have been preserved, as well as other idiosyncracies. In her manuscript copy, she tended in most cases to use the older English spelling of words. This *Walker's Dictionary* orthography has been honored here in the text, in spellings such as "endeavour" rather than "endeavor" (and honour, neighbour, practise, parlour, rumour, and so on).

The text has been transcribed from Emma's own handwritten copy of an earlier likely discarded diary that she kept as a teenager. In reminiscences written in old age, Emma mentioned that because her 1865 diary eventually began falling to pieces and "fading into illegibility" she decided to copy it, "or at least most of it." That copy, in which she included four pages of the original diary, forms the text of this book. It is not known when she made the copy, but a clue might be found in a label affixed to the binding, that of "B.R. Herty," a Milledgeville druggist and bookseller of the 1870s. Her handwritten copy, which has been digitized and can be viewed online, is part of the Southern Historical Collection at the Louis Round Wilson Special Collections Library at the University of North Carolina at Chapel Hill. Also available online is an electronic edition of a typewritten transcript of Emma's diary which was prepared as part of the Historical Records Survey of the WPA in 1938. There are several passages in Emma's copy that do not appear in the WPA transcript, and there are words and phrases in the WPA transcript that are not in Emma's copy. For instance, the name Quarterman was added in parentheses in the WPA version after the first names of two cousins,

Will and Joe Henry. Emma's copy made no such insertion. These have been identified in footnotes.

The version of Emma's diary that was published in 1957 as *When the World Ended* appears to be based on the WPA transcript. Edited by Earl Schenck Miers, it was regularized to modern punctuation and had frequent transcription errors and misidentifications. To give an example of one such transcription error, in Emma's entry for July 5, 1865, Emma's word "wholesome" was transcribed in the Miers edition as "welcome," resulting in a crucial distortion of meaning in an important passage describing a speech made by Colonel Haughton, the U.S. Army officer in charge of the occupation forces in Columbia, who was addressing a gathering of freed people, giving them, as Emma wrote, "wholesome advice." It was not likely that his advice was "welcome" to them, since he was known to be fair but firm in his dealings with the freed slaves, requiring them to work and remain orderly and peaceful. Emma noted that they disliked Haughton. Another occurred in the first paragraph where Emma's "moaning wind" became "morning wind." One misattribution was that of "Mr. Memminger," who was misidentified by the editor in a footnote as Christopher Gustavus Memminger, rather than his son Willis Memminger. Another significant error occurred when Emma mentioned "some of Foster's negro troops" and Miers' footnote misidentified the person referred to as General John A. Foster, Jr., rather than General John Gray Foster. Another was the confusion of Dr. Robert W. Gibbes with his son James.

The four original pages of the 1865 diary which Emma left in the recopied diary have been given precedence as copy text where there is any overlap or differences in the text of Emma's copy. For these four pages, the accidentals have been honored, in accordance with the editorial standards of the CEAA (Center for Editions of American Authors). The dashes, capitalization, spelling and punctuation here are closely in line with Emma's copied manuscript of the 1870s, and thus proves the latter to be a text loyal to Emma's original, and thus another reason for using her rewritten diary of the 1870s (in the absence of the first text) to provide the copy text of this edition.

The Diary of
Emma LeConte

Columbia, South Carolina,
Dec. 31st 1864

The last day of the year—Always a gloomy day—doubly so today! Dark leaden clouds cover the sky and the ceaseless pattering rain that has been falling all day. The air is chill and damp and the moaning wind fills one with melancholy—A fit conclusion for such a year! 'Tis fit old year that thou shoulds[t] weep for the misfortunes thou hast brought our Country! And what hope is there to brighten the New Year that is coming up? Alas—I can not look forward to the New Year—"My thoughts still cling to the Mouldering Past"[1]—Yes, the year that is dying has brought us more trouble than any of the other three long long years of this fearful struggle. Georgia has been desolated—The resistless flood has swept through that state, leaving but a desert to mark its preparing to hurl destruction upon the State they hate most of all, and Sherman the brute avows his intention of converting South Carolina into a wilderness.[2] Not one house, he says, shall be left standing, and his licentious troops—whites and negroes—shall be turned loose to ravage and violate. All that is between us and our miserable fate is a handful of raw militia assembled near Branchville.[3] And yet they may say there is a Providence who fights for those who are struggling for freedom— who are defending their homes, and all that is held dear!—Yet these vandals—these fiends incarnate, are allowed to overrun our land! Oh my country! Will I live to see thee subjugated and enslaved by these Yankees!—Surely every man and woman will die first. On every side they threaten—Lee's noble army alone stands firm—Foreign nations look on our sufferings and will not help us. Our men are being killed off—boys of sixteen are conscripted—Speculators and extortioners are starving us—But is this a time to talk of submission? Now when the Yankees have deepened and widened the breach by a thousand new atrocities? A sea rolls between them and us—a sea of blood. Smoking

---

1   A quote from Henry Wadsworth Longfellow's poem "The Rainy Day" (1842).
2   Emma as usual was accurate. Compare: "The Truth is, the whole army is burning with an insatiable desire to wreak vengeance upon South Carolina. I tremble at her fate." William Tecumseh Sherman to Chief of Staff, Gen. William Halleck, December 1860. The hatred of South Carolina was apparently there from the war's beginning. Mary Chesnut wrote that Horace Greeley in the *New York Tribune* wrote in 1861, "South Carolina is the meanest" state in the Union "and nobody will feel any compunction at laying it waste" (*Mary Chesnut's Civil War*, 214).
3   Sixty miles south of Columbia on the Charleston and Savannah Railroad.

houses, outraged women, murdered fathers, brothers and husbands forbid such a union. Reunion! Great heavens! How we hate them—with the whole Strength and depth of our Soul!

I wonder if the New Year is to bring us new miseries and sufferings! I am afraid so. We use to have bright anticipations of peace and happiness for the new year, but now I dare not look forward—Hope has fled, and in its place remains only a spirit of dogged sullen resistance.

* * *

January 1st 1865

What a bright new year! If only the sunshine be a presage of happier days! Cold but clear and sunny—such a contrast to yesterday's tears!— With this bright sun shining on me I can't feel as mournful as I did yesterday—I will try to throw off the sad memories I was brooding over and hope for better things—I will try to forget my struggles and failures and disappointments and begin again with new resolutions—Oh, me! I haven't much confidence in my ability to keep them!—

Yesterday we had a letter from my darling father—He was at Thomasville. He has been gone two weeks, and I suppose by this time he is at the Altamaha.[4] The Gulf Road only runs thus far, and there he will have to stop and get word if possible to Aunt Jane, with Sallie, Cousin Ada and Cousin Annie to meet him—[5] if that is impossible he will try to make

---

4   The Altamaha River in Georgia. While Sherman's armies were sweeping through Georgia, Professor LeConte traveled there to rescue his daughter Sallie, who was trapped behind enemy lines. A journal he kept of his harrowing adventures eluding the enemy army, which included several narrow escapes, was later published as *'Ware Sherman*. In February 1865, LeConte managed to make his way back to Columbia.

5   Emma's Aunt Jane Harden (1813-1876), Joseph LeConte's widowed sister, of Halifax Plantation 35 miles south of Savannah. Her daughters by John Berrien Harden (1810-1848) were Ada Louisa ("Cousin Ada," 1845-1930), Matilda Jane ("Cousin Tillie," 1837-1932), and "Cousin Annie" Harden. Jane's son was John Le Conte Harden (1839-1902), Emma's "Cousin Johnny" –and not to be confused with Emma's neighbor "Cousin Johnnie," her Uncle John and Aunt Josie LeConte's son, born in 1850. Emma wrote in her memoir in 1931: "We were all very fond of Aunt Jane." Aunt Jane Harden served as "surrogate mother" to both brothers Joseph and John LeConte (Stephens, *LeConte*, 12). Aunt Jane's husband, John M. Berrien Harden, was a former student of the naturalist John Edwards Holbrook at the College of Charleston and a significant contributor of specimens to Holbrook's work (Stephens, *Science*, 115). Sallie was Emma's fourteen year-old sister, Sarah Elizabeth (1850-1915), who was visiting her Aunt Jane. Emma wrote in her memoir, "We were always happy in Aunt Jane's house. She was always home to all of us." Of Cousin Ada, Emma wrote, "Our friendship had been growing as long as I could remember—strengthened each year by the regular winter visits." (Memoir, 8). Joseph arrived to find the Yankees had taken food, animals, and valuables, and destroyed furniture, but they did not burn the house or do harm to the ladies.

his way through the lines to them. Though I never say anything about it, I feel uneasy in regard to father. The Yankees have been through Liberty County, burning and destroying, and I hear they have passed right through our plantations. Father says however that he has heard of no outrages committed. But how dreadfully they must have been frightened. And what is worse, if the provisions have been destroyed, they may be suffering. The uncertainty is very horrible! But how accustomed we have grown to what is horrible!

We had a letter from Grandma too—[6] She had left us to be with Aunt Sallie in her confinement—[7] She gives a long account of her journey—performed mostly in Government wagons with wounded men. Poor Aunt Sallie suffered dreadfully, and her babe was born dead—the result of the fright she experienced when the enemy passed through Milledgeville.[8]

The old year did not die without bringing us one more piece of bad news—We heard yesterday that Gen Price—old "Dad Price"—was dead.[9] Misfortunes assail us on every side. The President however is quite well again. What a sinking of despair I had when I heard that he was dead.

Jan. 2nd

(This day's entry being filled with speculations on and arguments for and against the immortality of the soul, etc., I therefore extract only a short entry made before going to bed).

---

6   Emma's Grandmother Sarah Stillwell Nisbet, married to Alfred M. Nisbet of Athens, GA.

7   Grandma Nisbet's daughter and Joseph's sister-in-law, Sarah Angelina Nisbet (1834-1911), Emma's "Aunt Sallie." She was the widow of Joseph's oldest brother William LeConte (1812-1841). She remarried to a Mr. Moffett, then at his death, Edwin B. Weed in 1848. Weed had died in 1854, and she was thus twice widowed.

8   Sherman reached Milledgeville, Ga., on 23 November 1864.

9   General Sterling Price, defender of Georgia. The news she received was inaccurate. Price died in Missouri in 1867. Mary Boykin Chesnut received the same misinformation (*Chesnut Photograph Album*, 327).

Have just returned from Aunt Josie's,[10] where we spent the evening in company with Capt and Mrs Green—[11] We had a very pleasant evening and were regaled in honour of the New Year—which we celebrated today yesterday being Sunday—with egg nogg, Confederate cake and pop corn—Capt Green of the Nitre Bureau is an odd sort of man, and his wife is awfully ugly. No more news today except that I heard that Jeff Davis said that he would defend Carolina at all hazards—I hope it is true, but I do not believe it.

Jan. 4th

What a budget of bad news this morning!—Four letters—One from father who writes from camp at Doctorstown—only fifteen miles from Halifax, but he can not get there.[12] He had sent word to Aunt Jane by some scouts to try to reach him with the girls, but how can they when every mule and horse has been taken—they could only walk, and that of course would be impracticable. Father said the Yanks made a clean sweep of everything, and we have lost all our worldly possessions except the few negroes here. Perhaps Aunt Jane's family and Sallie are almost starving! Oh it is too dreadful to think of! A second letter from Aunt Ann in Baker County[13] says that Will and Joe Henry[14] seeing the outrageous conduct of the Yankees in one of the upper counties mounted and rode night and day to reach Liberty in time to beseech their mother and sisters to run anywhere rather than encounter such fiends. The house was surrounded (so says report)—Willie was killed Joe Henry mortally

---

10   Emma's Aunt Eleanor Josephine Graham LeConte (1824-1924), wife of John Eaton LeConte (1818-1891), Joseph's older brother. Emma's Aunt Josie was renowned for her beauty. She served as a member of the Ladies Hospital Association and a volunteer at the hospital in Columbia. The John LeContes lived at the corner of Sumter and Pendleton Streets in a two-storey brick house (the "Fourth Professor's House") built for them in 1860. The John LeConte house, now Flinn Hall, was moved from its site to its present location in 1934. In her memoir in 1931 Emma wrote "I had always been a pet of Aunt Josie. "
11   Dr. Allen J. Green, the post commander in Columbia. He had been the city's mayor in 1860 and oversaw the updating of the city's water system and other civic improvements. His Sumter Street home was burned by Sherman. He and Joseph Le Conte were in charge of the Confederate Nitre Bureau. They hid from Sherman in February 1865, and Joseph tells their exciting story in his war journal, '*Ware Sherman.*
12   In his autobiography, Joseph called Doctortown "the extreme outpost of the Confederate forces in that quarter and but twenty-six miles from Halifax [Plantation]" in Georgia.
13   Probably Ann Caroline Quarterman (born 1835), the daughter of Harriet Elizabeth Stevens Quarterman (Emma's "Aunt Harriet") and Joseph B. Quarterman (1796-1863).
14   Ann Quarterman's brothers, William James Quarterman (1846-1932) and Joseph Henry Quarterman (born 1843).

wounded, and Gus taken prisoner. Cousin Corinne's[15] husband was found in the swamp. How I hope it is not true—Poor Aunt Harriet![16] She has so recently buried her husband and daughter. And oh what are my feelings when I think of Aunt Jane, Annie and Ada and poor little Sallie! What fate may not have overtaken them, alone as they are upon the plantation![17] And father!—I can not bear to think of him—Every day I tremble with the fear that I may hear he is a prisoner or killed. Killed!—oh, no! God would not be so cruel as that—I could not think of that—My darling precious father if you were only safe at home again!

Grandma writes more dreadful accounts of outrages and horrors that happened in Milledgeville.[18] Walter[19] writes from the hospital in Charleston that he has been laid up with chills and fever as a consequence of the terrible march after the evacuation of Savannah. He has got transferred to our College hospital, and we expect to see him this evening—I am constantly thinking of the time when Columbia will be given up to the enemy—the horrible picture is constantly before my mind. They have promised to show no mercy in this State. Mother wants to send me off, but of course I would not leave her. I can only hope their conduct in a city will not be so shocking as it has been through the country. Yet no doubt the College buildings will be burned, with other public buildings, and we will at least lose our home.

15   Probably Harriet Stevens Quarterman's daughter.
16   Harriet Elizabeth Stevens Quarterman (1811-1887), wife of Joseph B. Quarterman. Not to be confused with another Aunt Harriet, Harriet Nisbet LeConte (1823-1892) of Athens, Georgia, wife of Joseph's brother Louis Eaton LeConte, Sr. (1821-1851). Joseph wrote in his autobiography that Louis "accidentally shot himself" and thus fell "victim of his passion for gunning."
17   See note 4. Joseph wrote in his autobiography that the women were there at Halifax Plantation "with no one to protect them but the negroes."
18   Newspapers reported a number of rapes committed by Sherman's soldiers in Milledgeville, Georgia. One young woman named Kate Latimer Nichols became insane as a result of the outrage and spent the rest of her life in an asylum. This incident was corroborated by a neighbor, Anna Maria Green, whose diary was published as *The Journal of a Milledgeville Girl, 1861-1867*.
19   Emma's cousin Walter Stevens (1847-1927) was the son of Joseph's sister Anne LeConte Stevens and J. P. Stevens. He came to live with Emma's family in Fall 1861 to attend college. Emma described him as "very bookish and something of a prig—most correct and stilted as to language" and "fresh from the country—with very little however of the country lad's vigour and sport" (Memoir, 4-5).

Jan. 6th

A horrid day—rain rain rain dark damp and dismal. I have been sitting over the fire knitting and reading—Mother sitting opposite with her knitting asked me such endless questions in regard to her stocking that I put down my book impatiently and am trying to write. I feel awfully cross and out of sorts, and can't at all understand how so simple an affair as knitting a stocking should appear an insoluble problem— Mother can't conquer the mystery of "turning the heel." There it is again. "Emma how many times did you say I must knit plain?"—I think I shall put my pen down and run away.————

It was brighter this afternoon in spite of the angry clouds—The sun was setting as we finished dinner and I brought my book out on the piazza where the rosy clouds divided my attention with the pages, when mother came and asked me to take Carrie.[20] I fear I did so ill-naturedly, but the little darling's laughing face and merry blue eyes soon put me in a better humour and I raced up and down with her till Jane came, when I ran upstairs, brushed my hair and coming down again found the moonlight struggling through the clouds.

Jan. 10th

What a day! The rain is sweeping down in torrents and the earth is flooded. Not a living creature to be seen—not even a benighted in the campus usually so alive with them—Nothing but the driving rain and rushing water. It is perfectly splendid!

* * *

---

20   Emma's little sister Caroline Eaton LeConte (1863-1945).

Jan. 12th

Last night Cousin Lula and Johnnie[21] came over and we all—Mother, Mr Memminger,[22] Walter, Cousin Lula, and myself—gathered round the table and made kiss verses all the evening for our Grand Bazaar. As might be supposed there was lots of nonsense and laughing over our work—if I except Walter who was silent as usual. I do not know what is the matter with him, he used to be so very talkative and now he is so gloomy—perhaps it is his health.

Troops have been passing through Columbia for some days and I feel a little safer, though if Joe Johnston is put in command we had as well pack up and prepare to run. He will certainly execute one of his "masterly retreats" from the coast back to Virginia, and leave us at Sherman's mercy. I hear that Sherman has drawn his troops back from S.C. to Savannah. Some think this bodes ill for Gen Hood[23] who is in Alabama or Mississippi or somewhere else, and may be caught in a trap between Sherman and Thomas.[24] I hope not. Cousin Lula says they had a letter from Julian yesterday. He, who was such an ardent Georgian, is down on the State for behaving so shamefully. He says all his company have abjured their State and made a vow never to live in it—especially in Savannah—As for me I am a South Carolinian—I have lived here almost

---

21   Emma's Cousin Lula (1843-1868) was the daughter of Joseph's brother John Eaton LeConte (1818-1891) and his wife Eleanor Josephine Graham Le Conte (Emma's "Aunt Josie"). Johnnie was John and Josie's son, born in 1850. Emma wrote in 1931 that Uncle John and Aunt Josie's eldest son Julian (nicknamed "Jule" or "Jules," 1845-1920) and his brother Johnnie were "more like brothers than cousins," and she and Cousin Lula became "close intimates" in spite of their age difference of four years. Emma wrote in her memoir that in March 1863, Julian, when he turned 18 years old, volunteered so as to enlist in their Cousin Johnny Harden's company, the Chatham Artillery, of Savannah "so I now had these two first cousins in the war—and in Aunt Josie's house there was anxiety" (Memoir, 28, 36). Emma's Aunt Josie was a favorite aunt, and Emma felt she was her "pet." They apparently had in common their devotion to the Confederate cause and their disdain for Sherman. Aunt Josie wrote a letter of 25 June 1866 to Wm. Sharswood that her husband had joined a commission to collect "all the testimony bearing upon the march of that fiercely incarnate fiend Sherman" and "a catalogue of crime will be laid at thy Door 'oh Union Savers'" (as quoted in Stephens, LeConte, 91, note 34.) Emma herself also uses the phrase "incarnate fiend" to describe Sherman in her diary.
22   In her memoir, Emma identified Mr. Memminger as Willis Memminger, son of Confederate Secretary of the Treasury Christopher Gustavus Memminger of Charleston. Emma wrote that Willis "beguiled the long evenings while Mother was engaged with the baby or otherwise, with his rather intelligent talk. We had great discussions on Science and Philosophy …He had quite a leaning to the occult & mystical, which rather amused me" (Memoir, 59-60). A note following the last diary entry in her copy states: "Willis Memminger son of Col. M., a personal friend of father's. He was with us before father left and seems still a member of the family."
23   John Bell Hood, who replaced General Johnston at Atlanta and then retreated to Nashville.
24   Virginia-born Union General George H. Thomas.

since I can remember, and only wish I had been born here instead of in Georgia! That whole State is utterly demoralized, and ready to go back into the union. Savannah has gone down on her knees[25] and humbly begged pardon of Father Abraham, gratefully acknowledging Sherman's clemency in burning and laying waste their State! Oh it is a crying shame—Such poltroonery!

* * *

Father writes that he will try to get them all out of Liberty Co under a flag of truce—I wish he would make haste and come home! Who can tell how soon communication may be cut off.

* * *

Jan. (between 13th & 17th)

We have no more news from father this morning, indeed there are no mails—The late freshet has carried away the bridges over the Edisto—the Greenville road is so injured that it can not be repaired under three weeks, and worse still the Danville road upon which Lee depends for his supplies can not be used for ten days and he is short of provisions. The very elements conspire against us!

Madame is going to make us repeat our comedy that came off with so much éclat in the Fall.[26] We rehearse this afternoon.

---

25   Savannah surrendered to Sherman on 22 December 1864 and he made a Christmas present of her to President Lincoln.

26   Madame Minde Zoe D'Ovilliers (1747-1888) was the widowed mother of teacher and artist Eugene A. D'Ovilliers (1818-1887), whom Emma described as "a very polished elderly Frenchman" who "taught the French Grammar and Reading" at Columbia Female Academy on Hampton Street. His father had been an engineer in the court of Napoleon Bonaparte until the fall of the empire. Emma described the Madame as "a dear little old lady something of a writer herself….She was very polite with our mistakes—much more so than we with hers when she tried to speak English." Emma identified the play as *L'Enfant Gate (The Spoiled Child)*. It was written by Madame D'Ovilliers (Memoir, 26, 53). The D'Ovilliers attended St. Peter's Catholic Church. According to Nell Graydon, Eugene D'Ovilliers had private pupils and also taught at Barhamville Academy and S.C. College. Their house sat at the northeast corner of Washington and Bull Street. The "lovely little house" survived the burning of the city and was sold by D'Ovilliers to Mary Hampton Manning in 1869. It was moved around 1960 "to an eastern suburb" (*Tales of Columbia,* 259). Edwin Scott wrote during the burning: "Went to Mr. D'Ovillier's [*sic*] and helped his wife put two or three big pictures in frames on her head, which she carried over to my house, and thence beyond the Female College, where her husband and his mother were in the street. Whilst there, [Prof. Charles] Pelham's house took fire, and with Dr. William Reynolds, Jr., I carried water from D'Ovillier's [*sic*] well to put it out. Brennan [Eugene's father-in-law], standing in Pelham's door, called on 3 or 4 soldiers in the street to assist in saving the building, but one of them said, 'damn the house, let it burn!' and they did nothing. It burnt and Sam Muldrow's next door" (*Random Recollections of a Long Life*, 180).

Wednesday [Jan.] 18th

Well our great bazaar opened last night, and such a jam![27] I was at the State House helping to arrange the tables until four o'clock so I was thoroughly tired. There are seven booths in the House. South Carolina at the Speaker's desk is the largest and on the other side Texas Tennessee Virginia Mississippi, Louisiana and Missouri. In the Senate are N. Carolina at the Desk, Arkansas, Georgia Alabama Florida. The tables or booths are tastefully draped with Damask and lace curtains, and elaborately decorated with evergreens. To go in there one would scarce believe it was war times. The tables are loaded with fancy articles—brought through the blockade or manufactured by the ladies—Everything to eat can be had if one can pay the price—cakes jellies creams candies—every kind of sweets abounds—A small slice of cake is two dollars—a spoonful of Charlotte Russe five dollars and other things in proportion. Some beautiful imported wax dolls not more than twelve inches high raffle for $500—and one very large doll I heard was to raffle for $2,000. Why, as Uncle John says,[28] one could buy a live negro baby for that! How can people afford to buy toys at such a time as this! However I suppose speculators can. A small sized cake at the Tennessee table sold for $75.

The Bazaar will continue until Saturday. They had intended holding it for two weeks but Sherman's proximity forces them to hurry up. I heard, but it is only one of Mr Johnston's stories, that the aforesaid individual had announced his intention of attending the Ladies' Bazaar in person before it closes. The railroads are so broken up that we can hear nothing definite but report says that Sherman is marching one column on Augusta and one on Branchville. One piece of bad news is certain, viz, that Fort Fisher has fallen at last.[29] I had expected to take great interest in the Soldier's Bazaar, but I can not—It seems like the dance of Death, and who can tell that Sherman may not get the money that was made instead of our sick soldiers! How long before our

---

27   On 17 January, each Southern state was represented against the red velvet curtains of the Hall of Representatives in the old state house. For sale were wedding rings, golden chains, and silver baby cups sent by mothers of dead sons. Nell Graydon wrote, "No possession was so dear that it was not willingly sacrificed by some mother or wife." (*Tales of Columbia*, 132).

28   Emma's Uncle John Eaton LeConte (1818-1891), Joseph's older brother, superintendent of the Works of the Confederate Nitre Bureau.

29   Fort Fisher, Wilmington, North Carolina, fell to Federal forces on 15 January 1865.

beautiful little city may be sacked and laid in ashes—dear Columbia with its lovely trees and gardens![30] It is heartsickening to think of it.— Grandpa[31] wants to leave for Georgia as soon as the trains run through which will be on Friday. And he wants to take me with him but I think mother and I had better stay or run together. We are going to pack up father's books and as many things as we can and get those of our friends who remain to take care of them as almost any house in the town will be safer than these buildings, then perhaps we may run with Uncle John's family to whatever point he moves the Nitre Bureau works—O it is so dreadful—And yet how callous our hearts have grown—Two years ago with what despair and agony I would have looked upon the prospect before us and now I only feel a dull heartsinking. If we were anywhere but in this State it would not be so horrible—but who can tell what will be our fate! O if father were only at home to advise us what to do. Sometimes I wonder I can be so calm—We have not heard from him in two weeks—he may be in Augusta or Branchville waiting to get through but if Sherman should reach those places before him and cut him off from us! Oh this fearful uncertainty is heartrending!—

Jan. 21st Sunday

News from father and Sallie at last!—They are safe, and I am so happy—how doubly happy now that I know that he has endured and escaped. He was a week in the County surrounded by Yankees—he

---

30   Emma was describing faithfully. David Conyngham, the correspondent for the *New York Herald* (12 March 1865) who followed Sherman's army, described Columbia similarly as being "famed for its fine public buildings, its magnificent private residences, with their lovely flower gardens which savored of Oriental ease and luxury." In 1853, Adam Summer called Columbia "that loveliest city of the South" and described its many double-lined avenues of oaks so that by 1853 the city had already become known as "The City of Magnificent Oaks." (*Southern Agriculturist*, 1 [September 1853], 259.) Blanding Street was lined in like manner with Southern Magnolias. There are various testimonies of Union soldiers to the beauty of the city's gardens. Several wrote in their diaries that they regretted the ashes in which they left the once beautiful streets. For example, Henry Wright of the 6th Iowa described the "loveliness and tropical splendor of the yards and grounds…with bowers of twining vines and flowering shrubbery." Samuel Byers of the 5th Iowa stated, "The beautiful gardens, flowers, trees and shrubbery for which the city was noted were all destroyed." William Gilmore Simms commented on the "umbrageous trees, set in regular order, and which, during the vernal season, confer upon the city one of its most beautiful features" (*Sack and Destruction*, 59). In 1860, novelist Joseph Holt Ingraham called Columbia "the paradise city of the South" (*The Sunny South; or, The Southerner at Home* [Philadelphia: Evans, 1860], 517). Several photographs of the city in 1865 and 1866 show the skeletons of burned street trees. For further treatment, see "'Oriental Luxury': The Gardens of Antebellum Columbia," *Magnolia*, 15 (Winter 1999), 11-14, and Kibler, "Columbia's Antebellum Ghost Gardens."
31   Alfred M. Nisbet, husband of Sarah Stillwell Nesbit.

walked 72 miles in three days—Sallie and Cousin Annie and Ada he sent out by a flag of truce.[32] Poor Sallie gives a dreadful account of her adventures—She walked half the distance of Doctortown camping out in the woods at night with no shelter, crossing burnt trestles and swollen streams on logs. Poor child! If they were only safe at home again—the nearer the time approaches the longer and more weary it seems. Father's letter was dated the 9th—Sallie's from Thomasville the 12th while they awaited a conveyance to take them to Albany, so as soon as the road is repaired (which it will be on Tues or Wed) I shall begin to hope for them. Sallie has been gone nearly three months and father five or six weeks.

A new trouble—Walter is down with the measles, and we fear if little Carrie should get them it will kill her in her delicate state of health. Mother is trying very hard to keep her from the infection.

* * *

Things are looking very gloomy. I heard Gov Magrath[33] had received orders to hold Charleston, but Mr M who was here yesterday says it is being evacuated. They say Richmond & Petersburg are to be given up and Lee's army fall back to South Carolina. That would be safer for us, but who could endure the idea of giving up Richmond! Glorious old Richmond that we have been defending so long—to fall after all those battles! That would be the darkest, darkest day of all.

Everyone seems to feel that Columbia is doomed—Aunt Josie thinks we had all better run off with the Nitre Bureau and camp in the woods of North Carolina till danger is over. They say Sherman is massing his forces at Branchville. Oh, what times to live in! Who knows what may become of us in ten days! Columbia is thought in so much danger that the ladies closed the Bazaar on Friday—Yet all this does not rouse us. We seem sunk in apathy—Nothing could surprise me now—unless some wonderful help should break in upon our trouble and give us the independence we have been longing and fighting for all these sad years—Even my books fail to keep my attention.

---

32 The WPA transcript here reads: "Sallie and Cousin Annie be sent out by a flag-of-truce." Miers modified this to "Sallie and Cousin Annie (are to) be sent out by a flag of truce."
33 Governor Andrew Gordon Magrath of Charleston.

22nd Jan

Mr Pond has arrived in Columbia with his command.[34] He says Butler's cavalry—5000 strong—will be stationed here for the present, so we will have some security at least from raids.[35] We can hear no news from the army except that Hood has been relieved of command at his own desire.—Taylor is in command pro tem.[36] No one seems to know the whereabouts of either Hood or Thomas. There is talk in Congress of making a Commander-in-chief and some recommend Joe Johnston. Gen Lee is the only man for that office.

[Jan.] 23rd

No more news from father. I begin to think he has stayed to get the negroes out—We hear so many rumours of the movement of the Yankees and of our own troops but they are worth nothing.

***

Mother has packed up the clothing and bed linen that we may save those at least. All the books are packed too. I have not been in the Library since they were taken down, it would make me too sad to look at the empty shelves.**I may be interested some day in recalling the poor style in which we lived during the war, so I shall make a few notes. My underclothing is of coarse homespun such as we gave the negroes formerly only much coarser. My stockings I knit myself and my shoes are of heavy calf skin. My dresses are two calicoes, a homespun, and an old delaine that hangs on in a dilapidated condition,[37] a reminiscence of better days. We have a couple of old silks carefully preserved for great occasions and which do not look shabby for the simple reason that all the other silks that still survive the war are in the same state of decay. The homespun costs about 8 or ten dollars a yard—calico is $20 or $30 a yard now, and going higher from week to week. My shoes are $150 dollars a pair. In two or three months these prices will be doubled. We live tolerably poorly. Two meals a day—Two plates of bread for breakfast—one of wheat flour, as five bags of flour were recently made

---

34   Possibly the Thomas Pond who was a colleague of John LeConte at Franklin College in 1853.
35   Matthew C. Butler, General Wade Hampton's top lieutenant, was with the rear squadron of Confederate cavalry.
36   Major General Richard Taylor, then stationed in Mississippi.
37   Delaine is a fine quality wool.

a present to us—else we would only have corn bread—Corn itself is $40 a bushel. Dinner consists of a very small piece of meat—generally beef, a few potatoes and a dish of hominy and a pone of corn bread. We have no reason to complain—So many families are so much worse off—Many have not tasted meat for months—And we too having a cow are able to have butter. Wood is hard to get at $100 a load. We keep but one fire—in the dining room where we sit. We have been fortunate in having gas thus far (at $80 a 1000 ft) but since the freshet the supply of rosin has been deficient and now and then it is cut off and we burn tallow candles at 2 dollars apiece—We never have sweet things now and even molasses candy is a rarity seldom to be thought of.

Jan. 25th

Last night while I was lying on the sofa feeling very blue and full of gloomy thoughts in regard to the war and the dreadful possibility of the South having to yield Uncle John came in the library and said "Well! Have you heard the last report? It is said that England [38] and France conjointly will certainly recognize us by the 4th of March."[39] I jumped up with the first thrill of real joy I have felt for a long time. A bright vista of peace and happiness seemed to open up before my "mind's eye." Of course a moment's reflection sobered me and brought me back to common sense. I recollected with a sigh how often we had been disappointed and lured on to false hopes by that will o'the wisp "Recognition and Intervention." Yet there are some circumstances that lend a slight colouring of possible truth to this rumour. Although at the height of their success, the Yankees are making fair proposals through their Commissioner Blair—if the South will only yield slavery.[40] Despatches say that much excitement prevails in Richmond, gold has

---

38   Southerners soon learned to call England "perfidious Albion" for her vacillation on recognizing the Confederacy as a country. The LeContes found such recognition particularly important because it would probably have lifted the blockade.

39   Throughout the war there were Confederate emissaries in Europe working to obtain foreign aid for and recognition of the Confederate States of America. In late 1864 President Jefferson Davis commissioned Duncan F. Kenner of Louisiana on a diplomatic mission to secure the official recognition of Great Britain and France on the condition that the Confederacy would emancipate the slaves. The purpose of Kenner's mission was supposedly secret, but in January 1865 Richmond newspapers were speculating about this eventuality.

40   Francis Preston Blair had acted as commissioner of the U. S. Government to negotiate a peace. President Jefferson Davis also appointed a commissioner to "secure peace to the two countries." Lincoln bristled and corrected to *our one common* country." Lincoln clearly did not want peace.

fallen, and the people are selling out. I think I would rather the South were conquered than that she should make peace with them!

* * *

Father has not come home yet, and we hear nothing! How tired we are of waiting—how I long to see them. Today is Johnnie's birthday—he is 15—Mother sent him one of our cobwebbed bottles of Champagne—a few still lurk in the pantry. I tell mother she must keep some for <u>peace</u> if we ever live to see it.

[Jan.] 27th

Another day and the long looked for have not returned.

* * *

Later

We have just received a letter from Sallie. She and cousins Annie and Ada are in Macon with our relatives while father has returned to attempt to save Aunt Jane by flag of truce.[41] Sallie entreats us to run if there is the slightest danger from Yankees. "Oh mother" she says, "I never want to see them again!" Cousin Ada in a letter to Aunt Josie gives a sad account of all they suffered and the brutal rudeness of the soldiers. I am so sorry for her—She and Aunt Jane are turned adrift homeless and destitute.

[Jan.] 28th

Grandpa leaves for Macon the day after tomorrow (Monday). Mother wanted to send me with him but we came to the conclusion that we had best not leave home or separate till father comes.

* * *

Mr Memminger was here this evening to bid us goodbye. He places no confidence in all our Recognition and Armistice rumours. He left early and a few minutes after Dr Nat Pratt dropped in and talked more cheeringly.[42] He seems quite confident we will hear tomorrow

---

41   Joseph's brother William and wife Sarah ("Aunt Sallie") Nisbet LeConte's daughter Annie (1836-1922), was married to Clifford Anderson. Cousin Ada Louisa Harden (1845-1930) was Aunt Jane Harden's daughter.
42   Dr. Nathaniel A. Pratt, chemist at the Confederate Nitre and Mining Bureau. After the

that an armistice of 60 days has been declared, having learned that Gen Hampton has received a telegram to that effect. Gen Lee has been made Generalissimo and Hood has taken leave of his army. His farewell address is very manly. He shoulders the whole responsibility of his campaign—Says he did his best and failed!—The weather is intensely—fearfully cold. Walter is getting on very well but is breaking out in boils now.

* * *

How dreadfully sick I am of this war! Truly we girls whose lot it is to grow up in these times are unfortunate! It commenced when I was thirteen—and I am now seventeen and no prospect yet of its ending! No pleasure—no enjoyment—nothing but rigid economy and hard work— nothing but the stern realities of life! Those which should come later are made familiar to us at an age when only gladness should surround us—We have only the saddest anticipations and the dread of hardships and cares when bright dreams of the future ought to shine on us. I have seen little of the lightheartedness and exuberant joy that people talk about as the natural heritage of youth—It is a hard school to be bred up in and I often wonder if I will ever have my share of fun and happiness! If it had not been for my books it would indeed have been hard to bear but in them I have lived and found my chief source of pleasure. I would take refuge in them from the sadness all around if it were not for other work to be done. I do all my own sewing now besides helping mother some. Now that everything is lost perhaps we will all have to work for a living before long. I would far rather do that and bear much more than to submit to the Yankees!

Jan. 29th Sunday

Dr Gibbes[43] said yesterday he was quite sure of the fact that Alex Stephens, J. R Campbell and R. M. T. Hunter had gone to Washington

---

war, Dr. Pratt went on to become a chemist with the Charleston Mining and Manufacturing Company.

43   Miers misattributes Dr. Gibbes as James G. Gibbes. He is probably either Columbian Dr. Robert Wilson Gibbes, South Carolina State Surgeon General and Pres. Thomas Cooper's assistant in chemistry at South Carolina College, or less likely, Robert's brother, Dr. Lewis R. Gibbes, professor at the College of Charleston and an eminent scientist. James Gujgnard Gibbes (1829-1903), Dr. Wilson's son, was never addressed as "Dr." Robert W. Gibbes (1809-1866) was a beloved physician, scientist, teacher, author, and journalist. His large and impressive brick home at the corner of Sumter and Hampton Street was burned by Sherman.

to treat for peace.[44] There is a general feeling throughout the South that we will have peace before long. There have been these national presentiments before however and I can not give much heed to this one. The whole atmosphere is filled with the wildest rumours. It is hard to study in the present state of affairs, and since father has been away I have only tried to read again. Yet in the uncertainty of everything I feel more than ever the pressing necessity of gaining an education and that I ought to try to persevere in working at it. I could not very well study physics and Latin while father is away, but I might finish Conic sections and review some Mathematics. All our future is so uncertain—We can not look beyond the present moment.

* * *

Jan. 31st

Just a month since I commenced writing—only a month yet how many changes even in that short time! Grandpa left us yesterday for Georgia.

* * *

I have just written again to Sallie. She may have left Macon before my letter reaches her but if not the poor child will be anxious enough for news from home. Walter[45] is a great trial to mother. He does not seem to feel her distress on account of his exposing little Carrie to the measles—We are terribly troubled about our little darling—She is so delicate and frail.

* * *

Simms wrote that this was the city's "most tragic cultural loss" owing to the destruction of Gibbes' large collections of fossils and Indian relics from the U. S. and Mexico, over 10,000 rare volumes, documents from the American Revolution, several hundred paintings from European Renaissance masters, American masters like Washington Allston and Thomas Sully, and an important collection of natural history (*Sack and Destruction*, 243). He saved only the clothes he was wearing and a bust of his little son, DeVeaux Gibbes, now at the Columbia Museum of Art. Gibbes died a year after Columbia burned at the age of 57 of poverty, exhaustion, and grief over the loss of so many family members.

44   Vice-president Alexander H. Stephens, Senator Robert M. T. Hunter, and Assistant Secretary of War John A. Campbell were the three Confederate peace commissioners who met with Abraham Lincoln and William H. Seward in early February 1865.

45   Emma's cousin Walter Stevens (1847-1927), son of Joseph's sister Anne.

Feb. 1st

What a delightful day it is! So balmy and delicious. It is almost oppressive in the sunshine and only the bare trees remind one that it is winter—it is one of those luxurious days that we often have in our Southern February, in which the warm sleepy air seems inviting to dreams and every sound has a softened far off cadence. Not a breeze is stirring and even animals seem to saunter along dreamily. What a climate would ours be were it not for these cold spells we have now and then! Sunday it was freezing, today it is Spring! I came out on the piazza to read, but fell to thinking instead of just such days two years ago. Cousin Annie[46] was here and how we wandered over the woods and the fields with Jules—sometimes sitting on the brown pine straw under that great old pine tree by the gurgling spring, talking lazily in the warm sunshine.[47] What a happy pleasant winter it was and how long ago it seems!

* * *

When shall we three meet again? Never under like circumstances. She is married and Julian in the army fighting for his country—I only am left in the old place.

* * *

We have received a letter from father at last! Is that not good news? But my poor darling father—what he has suffered! There were no Yankees this time but he had the elements to contend with and his sufferings were more than the last. It was during those terrible rains and for five days and nights he was on his feet, wet to the skin and sleeping in that condition—he worked like a negro—carrying Aunt Jane's[48] baggage and enduring every kind of fatigue—he crossed the Altamaha when it was so swollen by the freshet that experienced boatmen thought he risked his life.

* * *

What I dread is that he may yet be sick from the reaction. I reproach myself a thousand times that I have not felt more anxious about my

---

46   Aunt Jane Harden's daughter (1836-1922), married to Clifford Anderson of Macon, Ga.
47   Louis Julian (nicknamed "Jules" or "Jule," 1845-1920), the son of Joseph's brother John and Emma's "Aunt Josie."
48   Joseph's sister Jane Harden (1813-1876).

precious father but indeed we had not the slightest thought that he would meet with any obstacle this time.—Father said he would be home about the first so I look for him Friday or Saturday. How <u>will</u> I feel when they are all once more safe at home! I think my heart will overflow with joy and thankfulness.

Night

Still more rumours—peace rumours relative to the Blair Mission and our own Commissioners in Washington.[49] I am not hopeful but every one around me seems so confident that I can not help being infected more or less with the general feeling. People seem looking very eagerly to European intervention.

* * *

Feb. 2nd Thursday

I can not expect it yet I do hope the long watched for will come tonight. It is almost impossible, yet I long for them so. Not only to feel that father were safe at home—that were a weight off one's heart—but there is another anxiety now. Little Carrie has the measles—Dr. Thomson said so this morning and we are so distressed about it.[50] I am so anxious about my little darling and so sorry father will find her sick. She has been so well since he left till now.

* * *

Sunday Feb. 5th

A rainy day and consequently neither mother nor I went to church.[51] Last evening Mrs Caldwell [52] sent word that her father had seen Dr Le

---

49   In January 1865 Lincoln's adviser Francis Preston Blair, Sr. met with President Jefferson Davis, and an agreement was reached to send commissioners to what would become known as the Hampton Roads Conference, where Confederate officials, including Vice President Alexander H. Stephens, met with President Lincoln and U.S. Secretary of State William Seward. This "peace conference" which took place on 3 February 1865, ended in failure.
50   Dr. Andrew Wallace Thomson (1827-1881), a surgeon at the Confederate hospital on the South Carolina College campus.
51   First Presbyterian Church, Sumter Street, Columbia.
52   This is likely Mrs. Agnes Montague Caldwell, the widow of Howard Hayne Caldwell (1831-1860), a lawyer and poet, born in Newberry District, South Carolina. She was the daughter of Charles Montague, a native of Ireland, and the 1860 census lists her as living in his

Conte in Macon, and that he bade him tell us he would start home in a few days. I put on my hat and shawl and ran around there to learn something more definite but Mrs C. could not even tell me what day her father was in Macon, but only that he said father looked quite well but sunburnt from exposure. As I returned I stopped to chat with Cousin Lula[53] on the piazza and lingered so long that the rest of my walk home was thro the moonlight—it was so lovely and the air so soft and balmy. We can not think what could detain father in Macon.

* * *

Uncle John thinks the train may come through today. If not father may take a government wagon from Augusta in which case we may expect him Tuesday or Wednesday.

* * *

He may return just in time for us to take a toilsome flight for the present plan seems to be to run if the Yankees come. After the threats uttered in Georgia against this State it would seem folly to remain—So we propose to accompany the Bureau. Aunt Josie says Uncle John is putting springs in some of the wagons for our accommodation—We are to travel out of the track of the enemy and stop at some little village until Columbia is out of danger, or until it is decided where the Nitre Bureau will be located. We will carry bedding and impress provisions at Government prices for the Bureau. This will be quite an expedition—

* * *

But I so dread leaving home—for I feel I would never see it again except in ashes. How one grows accustomed to things! A year ago all this would have made me half crazy with anxiety and excitement—now it seems natural. We are prepared for the worst and dare not look even into the immediate future. I can not even attempt to picture to myself what may happen in the next six weeks, or what may be the fate of our dear beautiful old Columbia.

* * *

---

residence in Columbia. She had at least two younger sisters named Francena (or Frances) and Ellen (or "Nellie").
53   John LeConte's daughter (1843-1868), living at the "Fourth Professor's House" at the southeastern corner of Pendleton and Sumter streets.

At church this afternoon Dr Palmer[54] said that an ambulance train was to be sent to Branchville and necessary supplies for the wounded were solicited from the ladies—I stopped at Aunt Josie's coming back to see how Johnnie[55] got on with the measles and found him up. Uncle John says in a day or two the town will be flooded with the wounded—that there will not be sufficient hospital accommodation, and that private houses will have to be opened to receive them. Alas! the horrors of war are coming home to us now. Our College hospital has indeed always been full, and the disabled limping soldier has grown to be as familiar as was formerly the festive student in these classic grounds. But we have never yet been literally surrounded by the wounded, the dead and dying.

* * *

Sometimes I still try to get away from all the horrid present by forgetting myself in a book—I have been reading just now Hitchcocks Religion and Geology.[56] I find a good many ideas there that Mr M[57] in our talks advanced as his own—sometimes expressed in the identical words—I think he had very recently read the book. By the way, M. left Columbia the other day—It is not likely we will ever be thrown together again—Well, I had a very pleasant time with him while he was here. He is right clever, has read a good deal and his wild theories and still wilder dreams amuse and entertain me.

7th Feb. Tuesday

What gloomy weather it is—the rain is flooding down in torrents. I would not mind the pouring rain, but that my imagination pictures

---

54   The Reverend Dr. Benjamin Morgan Palmer. Emma described him as "a man of vivid imagination and an unusual flow of language." (Memoir, 64). Thomas Elmore in *Days of Destruction* noted he was an avid secessionist in New Orleans and was successful in urging the state of Louisiana out of the Union. When New Orleans fell in 1862, he had to flee for his life. He had preached at First Presbyterian in Columbia before going to New Orleans. From New Orleans he returned to Columbia, but again had to flee "to avoid capture and possible death." In the burning of the city, he lost his house and all his books and papers. Palmer returned to Columbia in March 1865. (Elmore, 189, 509).
55   Aunt Josie's son John, born in 1850.
56   Edward Hitchcock's *The Religion of Geology and Its Connected Sciences* (1851). Emma's father had given Sunday lectures in Columbia on religion and science, reconciling the theory of evolution with Christian belief. LeConte accepted Darwin's theory. He collected these essays as *Religion and Science* (1873), his first published book. Emma later laments not having her father to help her with the book's "metaphysical portion" (Diary, 8 March). See also Note 115.
57   Willis Memminger.

father and the rest exposed to its fury—perhaps in an open government wagon. We hoped for them a little yesterday—would look for them certainly tonight but that we have been so often disappointed.

* * *

All this continual fear and anxiety have made me realize how intensely I love my dear precious father.

* * *

Walter[58] has just returned from the Medical Board where he went to secure a sick furlough—he will probably be successful.

* * *

The hospital is to be moved to North Carolina as Columbia is in danger—our own movements are unsettled, so altogether he prefers going home to S.W. Georgia.

* * *

Wed. [Feb.] 8th

Joy, joy! They have come. Last night when I met father I think I was perfectly happy.

* * *

I was standing downstairs in the basement by the fire (Mother & I have moved down there since Carrie's illness) when I heard a step in the hall. "It is father" I thought, then I tried to persuade myself it was only Walter—then I heard someone descending the stairs—I ran to the door to find my eager hope realized. With a cry of joy I threw myself in father's arms and clung to him kissing him. He was wet through—hair and beard dripping. After a few moments he went back to Aunt Josie's and fetched Sallie over, who received a glad welcome home. Then such talking! But another time I will try to give some account of their adventures.

* * *

About ten o'clock this morning, Walter having just left us, I went over to Aunt Josie's to see Aunt Jane and Cousin Ada.

---

58   Emma's cousin Walter Stevens.

Feb. 9th

I went to Aunt Josie's to return a glove pattern and to carry over some of Aunt Jane's things that were with Sallie's. Found them all well.

* * *

Father is not well however; his return to the house, after his open air life has given him a severe cold.

* * *

He and mother agree to let me teach Sallie, both that she may be studying and that I may learn to teach.

Saturday [Feb.] 11th

I hardly know where to begin my journal of yesterday, so many things happened—To begin with the morning—While at the breakfast table Peter came in from Aunt Josie's to tell us that Jule and Cousin Johnnie had just arrived.[59] Imagine our surprise! Shortly afterwards father received an order from Richmond to pack up and move the laboratory to Athens Ga. For a while we of course supposed we would go also—even now it seems probable. So here was abundant subject for thought and talk. To think that we should really have to set to work immediately to pack up and leave home was enough to keep our brains active—

* * *

Returning from my French lesson I stopped at Aunt Josie's to find her half crazy with delight at having Jule again—And Aunt Jane equally happy but not quite so overcome. While both boys looked as large and natural as life—They had burst into the house about 8 a.m. without a word of warning. Fancy Aunt Josie's joy at seeing her soldier boy after more than a year's absence during which time his life has been constantly exposed. Julian is not quite so stout as he was a year ago last Christmas—his beard is quite formidable and altogether he is a very handsome soldier. Cousin Johnny is somewhat changed but looks well.

59　Emma's Aunt Jane Harden's son was "Cousin Johnny" (1839-1902), here uncharacteristically spelled "Johnnie," and spelled "Johnny" below. Jule was Julian, son of John and Josie LeConte, who joined Cousin Johnny Harden's Company, the Chatham Artillery of Savannah in March 1863 when he became 18 years old.

Their battery is to remain here for the present—to be mounted and then to join Hampton. Father telegraphed Col St John[60] to know if he must accompany the laboratory to Athens—he has not yet received an answer but since he is consulting chemist he will probably be kept on the line of the telegraph, the two laboratories being consolidated under Pratt. Still he may be ordered to Georgia. It is very hard for me to think of leaving home—Yet the town is in such danger, and we feel so restless.

* * *

12th or 13th [Feb.]

Father brought in some news this morning—First and worst. The Yankees are skirmishing at Orangeburg—Second and more encouraging—Gen Hampton says Sherman will not come to Columbia— At all events we certainly will know in a day or two what he is going to do. Mr Walker has been taking steps toward boxing up and sending off the Library but the Governor does not think he can obtain transportation for such a large collection of books.

* * *

Feb. 14th Tuesday

What a panic the whole town is in![61] I have not been out of the house myself, but father says the intensest excitement prevails on the Streets. The Yankees are reported a few miles off on the other side of the river— how strong no one seems to know. It is decided if this be true, that we will remain quietly here, father alone leaving. It is thought Columbia can hardly be taken by a raid as we have the whole of Butler's cavalry here, and if they do we have to take the consequences. It is true some think Sherman will burn the town, but we can hardly believe that— Besides these buildings, though they are state property, yet the fact that they are used as a hospital will, it is thought, protect them. I have been hastily making large pockets to wear under my hoopskirt—for

---

60   Col. Isaac M. St. John, Confederate Chief of the Nitre and Mining Bureau in Richmond, Va.
61   Joseph LeConte noted in his autobiography, "The depot was crowded with people trying to get away, women and children pleading to be taken aboard the cars. The panic was really frightful, but still I strove to remain calm." He concluded, the "first and second lines of our defense" were gone and "the booming of the enemy's guns sounded ever nearer and nearer."

they will hardly search our persons.[62] Still every thing of value is to be packed up to go with father. I do not feel half so frightened as I thought I would—perhaps because I can not realize they are coming—I hope still this is a false report. Maggie Adams[63] and her husband have promised to stay here during father's absence—she is a Yankee and may be some protection and help—Our sufferings will probably be of short duration, as they will hardly send more than a raid—they would not have time to occupy the town—But I can not believe they are coming!

* * *

Aunt Josie and all will remain I suppose—indeed they would not have time now to put into execution their projected flight. Alas! What may we not have gone through with by the end of this week! Ah! me I look forward with terror and yet with a kind of callousness to their approach.

Night

Father says the above is a false alarm. It was only a raid of 300 men which was repulsed by our forces. The evil day is at least postponed.

Wednesday [Feb.] 15th

Oh how is it possible to write amid this excitement and confusion! We are too far off to hear and see much down here in the Campus, but they tell me the streets in town are lined with panic stricken crowds trying to escape—All is confusion and turmoil—the government is rapidly moving off stores—all day the trains have been running, whistles blowing and wagons rattling through the streets—All day we have we have been listening to the booming of cannon—receiving conflicting rumours of the fighting—All day wagons and ambulances have been bringing in the wounded over the muddy streets and through the drizzling rain, with the dark gloomy clouds overhead. All day in our own household has confusion reigned too—The back parlour strewed

---

62   For once, Emma erred. In haste to take jewelry, soldiers sometimes even ripped earrings from ladies' ears, so that the lacerated lobes of Columbia ladies became the symbol of the war for Hanoverian diplomat August Conrad, who saw a lady with her earlobes torn apart. See also Simms, *Sack and Destruction*.
63   Possibly Margaret Crawford Adams. She and her family were able to flee the town to Winnsboro, South Carolina. In *South Carolina Women in the Confederacy*, Adams has a touching remembrance of the invasion (209-224).

with clothing etc. etc.—open trunks standing about, while a general feeling of misery and tension pervades the atmosphere. Everything is to go that can be sent—house linen, blankets, clothing, silver, jewelry, even the wine—everything movable of any value. Hospital flags have been erected at the different gates of the Campus—We hope the fact of our living within the walls may be some protection to us—but I fear not—I feel sure these buildings will be destroyed—I wish mother could have sent some furniture to different friends in town, but it is too late now. Aunt Josie has sent her pictures, Uncle John's manuscripts and some clothing to the Roman Catholic priest house on Main St—Aunt Jane was here a few moments ago with Cousin Ada—She advised mother as to what things she had better send off—She says Aunt Josie is in a dreadful state of excitement. Neither mother nor I are much alarmed though poor Sallie is much frightened and has been crying hysterically all the morning. I have destroyed most of my papers but have a lot of letters still that I do not wish to burn, and yet I do not care to have them share the fate of Aunt Jane's and Cousin A's in Liberty Co which were read and scattered along the roads.[64] I will try to hide them—One of my bags is filled—the other I will pack tonight. Henry will stay with us and vows he will stand by us through thick and thin—I believe he means it, but do not know how he will hold on. It is so cold and we have no wood—The country people will not venture in town lest their horses should be impressed. So we sit shivering and trying to coax a handful of wet pine to burn—

* * *

Yonder come more wounded — poor fellows! Indeed I can write no more—

Night

Nearer and nearer, clearer and more distinctly sound the cannon—O it is heart sickening to listen to it! For two or three hours after dinner the cannonade ceased, but for a half an hour past, at short intervals the same sounds with the roar of musketry break upon us frightfully near and sounding above the din of a tumultuous town and above the rattling

---

64   Mrs. Louisa McCord's papers were scattered in the same way at her home across from the college in Columbia.

carts. Just now as I stood on the piazza listening, the reports sounded so frightfully loud and near that I could not help shuddering at each one. And yet there is something exciting, sublime in a cannonade—But the horrible uncertainty of what is before us! My great fear now is for father—Oh! if he were only gone! Were only safe!

The alarm bell is ringing. Just now when I first heard it clang out my heart gave a leap and I thought at once, "It is the Yankees!" So nervous have I grown that the slightest unusual sound startles me. Of course I knew it was a fire, yet it was with a beating heart I threw open the window to see the western horizon lit up with the glow of flames.[65] Although we are composed, our souls are sick with anxiety.

* * *

O if father were only safely off!

I try to be hopeful, but if it is true as it is now said, that this is one of Sherman's Army Corps, what resistance can one handful of troops make. Oh! if Cheatham's corps would only come![66] Beauregard said he was expecting it in 15 hours, and that was about 2 p.m. They should therefore be here early tomorrow morning. Will they come! Oh if Columbia could only be saved. They surely ought not to give it up without a struggle.[67]

Later

They have passed our first line of breastworks. No firing tonight. Father and Uncle John leave tonight or tomorrow morning.

Thursday [Feb.] 16th

How can the terror & excitement of today be described! I feel a little quieter now and seize the opportunity to write a few lines. Last night, or rather early this morning father left. After the last lines in my entry for last evening, I went downstairs and found in the back parlour a man calling himself Davis.[68] I had heard father speak of him before—He met

---

65   The glow was from Sherman's burning of the town of Lexington and its county courthouse, due west of Columbia.
66   A corps of the Army of Tennessee under the command of Maj. Gen. Benjamin Cheatham.
67   General Beauregard was given command of all troops in South Carolina on 15 February 1865. Confederate Gen. Benjamin Cheatham did not arrive.
68   The mysterious Charles Davis, either a Confederate spy or double agent. Joseph's most

him in Georgia while making his way home with Sallie and he was very kind to them during that difficult journey. He calls himself a Confederate spy or scout and is an oddity—I only half trust him—he evidently is not what he pretends to be. He says he is a Kentuckian and is both coarse and uneducated, but wonderfully keen and penetrating. He talked a great deal and entertained us by reading our different characters for us. He has taken an unaccountable fancy to father—as shown by his hunting him up—And he assures him again and again that he will have us protected during the presence of the Yankees here. He claims great influence with the Yankee officers and entire knowledge of the enemy's movements. All the evening he seemed exceedingly uneasy that father should so long have deferred his departure and very impatient to get him off. He offered to lend him a horse if that would facilitate his leaving—Father is not uneasy for our authorities assure him that it is all right—but I do not like this man's evident anxiety. Can he know more than our generals? At about 12 ½ father took leave of us. Thus to part!— Father starting on an uncertain journey—not knowing whether he may not be captured in his flight and leaving us to the mercy of the inhuman beastly Yankees. I think it was the saddest moment of my life. Of course father feels very anxious about us and the last words the man Davis said to him were to assure him that he might feel easy about us—I wonder if there is any confidence to be put in what he says! hardly I suppose. We said goodbye with heavy hearts and with many presentiments of evil. After father was gone I sat up still, talking with Davis—I could not sleep and besides I wanted to hear that father was safely off. We asked our guest how he thought Columbia would be treated—he said he would not tell us—it would alarm us too much—Does he really know all he pretends, or is he only guessing? It was three o'clock before I lay down and fell into a disturbed doze which lasted till seven. Davis stayed and slept on the ground floor, but was gone before we awoke.

The breakfast hour passed in comparative calm. About 9 o'clock we were sitting in the Dining room, having just returned from the piazza

---

extensive account of Davis appears in his '*Ware Sherman*. Twenty-year-old Davis said he was from Kentucky, a member of Lewis' Kentucky Cavalry, was using an assumed name, and had fought the Yankees with Wheeler all through Georgia. He appeared at the LeContes on the 15th. He had been sent to town to arrest a female Yankee spy and "a citizen of this place." He told Joseph that the city would be burned the following day and that he would try to protect his and his brother John's houses during the burning (75-77, 83-84.)

where we had been watching a brigade of cavalry passing to the front. "Wouldn't it be dreadful if they should shell the city!" Someone said. "They would not do that," replied Mother, "for they have not demanded its surrender." Scarcely had the words passed her lips when Jane the nurse[69] rushed in crying out that they were shelling. We ran to the front door just in time to hear a shell go whirring past.[70] It fell and exploded not far off—This was so unexpected. I do not know why, but in all my list of anticipated horrors I somehow had not thought of a bombardment. If I had looked for it I wouldn't have been so frightened. As it was for a few minutes I leaned against the door fairly shivering, partly with cold, but chiefly from nervous excitement. After listening to them awhile this wore off and I became accustomed to the shells. Indeed we were in no immediate danger, for the shells were thrown, principally, higher up. They were shelling the town from Lexington heights just over the river, and from the Campus gate their troops could be seen drawn up on the hilltops.

Up the street this morning, the government stores were thrown open to the people and there was a general scramble—Our negroes were up there until frightened home by the shells. The shelling was discontinued for an hour or two and then renewed with so much fury that we unanimously resolved to adjourn to the basement and abandon the upper rooms. Sallie and I went up to our rooms to bring down our things. I was standing at my bureau with my arms full, when I heard a loud report. The shell whistled right over my head and exploded. I stood breathless, really expecting to see it fall in the room. When it had passed I went into the hall and met Sallie, coming from her room, pale and trembling. "O Emma" she said, "this is dreadful"—

We went downstairs—Mother stood in the hall looking very much frightened—"Did you hear?"—"Yes indeed" and at that instant another whistled close overhead. This was growing rather unpleasant and we retreated to the basement without further delay, where we sat listening,

---

69   Likely, one of three named slaves living with the LeContes. Henry, Joseph's manservant, and his wife Mary Ann, the cook, were the others. The LeContes employed white servants as well, so there is an outside possibility that Jane was not a slave.
70   The LeConte home was a short three blocks from the State House, which was the sighting target of the Union artillery on the Lexington (western) side of the river. The house would have been exposed directly in the line of sight of the cannons, and it is no wonder that shells went whizzing by. Today, several bronze stars mark the spots where cannon balls struck the State House in that line of site.

as they fell now nearer and now farther off—Sallie suffered most—she would not be left alone, and would not allow me to go to the outer door to look about but would call me back in terror. The firing ceased about dinner time, but as may be imagined none of us could eat. During the afternoon a rapid cannonade was kept up and I do not think the forces could not have been more than a half a mile from here—Dr. Thomson says they are only skirmishing. Davis says we have received reinforcements—but he thinks we can not hold the town as we have given up the strongest position. He was here this morning during the shelling and stood talking to me in the dining room for some time giving me a picture of the confusion up town—One soldier had opened and plundered some of the stores—He brought me a present of a box of fancy feathers and one or two of the little things he had picked up. He says the bridge will be burned and the town evacuated tonight.

10 o'clock p.m.

They are in bed sleeping or trying to sleep—I don't think I shall attempt it. Davis was here just now to tell us the news—it is kind of him to come so often to keep us posted. I went up to see him—made Henry[71] light the gas[72] and sat talking to him in the hall, while through the open door came the shouts of the soldiers drawn up along the streets ready to march out—Perhaps the Yankees may be in tonight—The dreadful hour is very close on us—yet I do not feel as frightened as I thought I would. Dr Thomson[73] reassures us—he does not think we will suffer half as much as we imagine. Maggie is not coming—we three will have to tough

---

71   Described by Joseph LeConte as "my faithful man-servant" who helped Mrs. Le Conte move valuables to the back garden when his brother John's house at the corner of Sumter and Pendleton was set on fire several times. Joseph continued that his wife wrapped Carrie in a blanket "and carried her in her arms fast asleep…far into the back garden, where she and all the children remained a considerable portion of the dreadful night" ('*Ware Sherman*, 142). Henry apparently had a room of his own in or behind the LeConte house in a two-storey detached structure that also served as the kitchen. Emma described him as hiding "in his room" to avoid being forced to go with the soldiers. His wife was Mary Ann, the family cook and primary house servant, whom Joseph and Bessie had raised as an orphan.

72   Natural gas first came to South Carolina in Charleston in 1846. Columbia had installed a gas works under the direction of George E. Walker in the 1850s.

73   Andrew Wallace Thomson (1827-1881), a Confederate surgeon who remained with the campus hospital where there were "180 or 190 sick and dying." William A. Nicholson describes how the pitiful, frightened sick and dying tried to escape the flames by dragging themselves out onto the campus green (Nicholson, in Stokes, *A Legion of Devils*, xii-xiv). Emma's father noted "the patients were all moved out into the open area in the middle of the campus, and more than twenty of them died next day in consequence of exposure and fright." ('*Ware Sherman*, 142)

it out alone. We have moved into the back basement room—I opened the door, which goes from our present sleeping room on the back yard, just now and the atmosphere was stifling with gunpowder smoke. After I left Davis and came downstairs a while ago the gas went out so I am writing now by the firelight. I suppose it will be several days before we see gas again. Fortunately mother has a few candles. Henry had to cut down a tree in the yard today to furnish us with fuel.

But I must put by my pencil for tonight. I wonder what I will have to write about next time! Oh! If I could only guess what is to be our fate!

* * *

Friday [Feb.] 17th

How long is this distress of mind to continue? It is now about 11 o'clock and it is the longest morning I ever passed. I threw myself on the bed late last night or rather early this morning without undressing, feeling that if I did not take some rest I would be sick. It was some time before I could sleep as every now and then a cannon report would break the stillness. So in spite of my heavy eyelids I lay awake thinking of the dreadful possibility of the town's being shelled in the night and also of the tumult I knew was reigning up town. At last I fell into a heavy sleep. It was about 6 o'clock, still quite dark & all in the room were buried in profound slumber when we were suddenly aroused by a most terrific explosion. The house shook and a broken window frame fell on the floor. We started up frightened half to death. My first impression from awaking was that the house had been struck by a shell, but as soon as I recovered my senses I knew no shell could make such a noise. We lit the candles & sent Jane to inquire of Henry the cause of it—He did not know. The day was beginning to break & the air out of doors was still filled with smoke. All continued quiet and we came to the conclusion that the authorities had blown up some stores before evacuating. Whatever the cause, the effect was to scare us very effectually and to drive away all thought of sleep. We got up an hour later almost fainting, for we had eaten almost nothing the preceding day. I forced myself to eat a little and to drink a half a cup of coffee. After breakfast the cannon opened again and so near that every report shook the house—I think it must have been a cannonade to cover our retreat—It did not continue very long. The negroes all went up town to see what they could get in the general pillage, for all the shops had been opened and provisions were scattered in all directions.

Henry says in some parts of Main St corn and flour and sugar cover the ground. An hour or two ago they came running back declaring the Yankees were in town and that our troops were fighting them in the streets. This was not true, for at that time every soldier nearly had left town—but we did not know it then. I had been feeling wretchedly faint and nauseated with every mouthful of food I swallowed—And now I trembled all over and thought I should faint—I knew this would not do, so I lay down awhile and by dint of a little determination got quiet again. Mother is downright sick—She had been quite collected and calm until this news but now she suddenly lost all self control and exhibited the most lively terror—indeed I thought she would grow hysterical. As for Sallie her fright may be more easily imagined than described. This condition of affairs only lasted about half an hour but it was dreadful while it did last. As soon as I could I put on my pockets and nerved myself to meet them—but by and by the firing ceased and all was quiet again. It was denied that the Yankees had yet crossed the river or even completed their pontoon bridge and most of the servants returned up town. They have brought back a considerable quantity of provisions— The negroes are very kind and faithful—they have supplied us with meat and Jane brought mother some rice and crushed sugar for Carrie knowing that she had none. How times change! Those whom we have so long fed and cared for now help us.

* * *

We are intensely eager for every item of news, but of course can only hear through the negroes—A gentleman told us just now that the mayor had gone forward to surrender the town.

1 o'clock p.m.

Well they are here! I was sitting in the back parlour, when I heard the shouting of the troops—I was at the front door in a moment. Jane came running and crying, "O Miss Emma, they've come at last!" She said they were marching down Main Street, before them flying a panic stricken crowd of women and children who seemed crazy. As she came along by Aunt Josie's, Miss Mary[74] was at the gate about to run out. "For God's sake Miss Mary" she cried "stay where you are!" I suppose she (Miss M.) thought of running to the convent. I ran upstairs to my bedroom window, just in time to see the U.S. flag run up over the State House.[75] O what a horrid sight! What a degradation—to see it over the capitol of South Carolina—After four long bitter years of bloodshed and hatred—now to float there at last!—that hateful symbol of despotism! I do not think I could possibly describe my feelings—I know I could not look at it. I left the window and went back downstairs to mother. In a little while a guard arrived to protect the hospital. They have already fixed a shelter of boards against the wall near the gate—Sentinels are stationed and they are cooking their dinner—The wind is very high today and blows their hats around. This is the first sight we have had of these fiends except as prisoner—the sight does not stir up very pleasant feelings in our hearts—we can not look at them with anything but horror and hatred, loathing and disgust.—The troops now in town is a brigade commanded by Col Stone.[76] Everything is quiet and orderly—Guards have been placed to protect houses and Sherman has promised not to disturb private property. How relieved and thankful we feel after all our anxiety & distress!

Later

Gen. Sherman has <u>assured</u> the mayor "that he and all the citizens may sleep as securely and quietly tonight as if under <u>Confederate</u> rule. Private property shall be carefully respected—Some public buildings have to be destroyed, but he will wait until tomorrow when the wind shall have entirely subsided."—It is said that one or two stragglers from

---

74 This was likely Mary ("Mollie") Graham, the sister of Aunt Josie. Her home was in the North but she was in Columbia when the war began and was unable to return home until after the war. See *Women of the Civil War South: Personal Accounts from Diaries, Letters and Postwar Reminiscences,* 2003, by Marilyn M. Culpeper.

75 Several eye-witness illustrations of this event reveal the accuracy of Emma's description. One shows the 13th Iowa Regiment of the 17th Corps raising the flag. The giant 14 by 36 foot South Carolina Palmetto flag which had flown there was taken by troops of the 13th and 15th Iowa regiments. It resides in Iowa, in storage at the Iowa Historical Society, which refuses to return it to South Carolina. On 16 February 1990, Rodger Stroup, director of the South Carolina State Museum, borrowed the flag and restored it at South Carolina's expense before returning it to Iowa.

76 George A. Stone, commander of a brigade of the 15th Corps which consisted of Iowa regiments.

Wheeler's command fired on the flag as it was borne down Main St on the carriage containing the mayor, Col. Stone and the officers.

Saturday afternoon [Feb.] 18th

What a night of horror misery and agony! It is so useless to try to put on paper any idea of it—The recollection of it is so fearful—yet any attempt to describe it seems so useless—It even makes one sick to think of writing down such scenes—And yet as I have written thus far, I ought while it is still fresh, try even imperfectly to give some account of last night. Every incident is now so vividly before me and yet it does not seem real—rather like a fearful dream or nightmare that still oppresses.

Until dinner time we saw little of the Yankees, except the guard about the campus, and the officers and men galloping up and down the street. It is true, as I have since learned, that as soon as the bulk of the army entered, the work of pillage began.[77] But we are so far off and so secluded from the rest of town that we were happily ignorant of it all. I do not know exactly when Sherman entered but I should judge about two or between one & two p.m. We could hear their shouts as they surged down Main St. and through the State House but were too far off to see much of the tumult, nor did we dream what a scene of pillage and terror was being enacted—I hear they found a picture of President Davis in the capitol, which was set up as a target and shot at amid the jeers of the soldiery. From three o'clock till seven their army was passing down the street by the campus, to encamp back of us in the woods. Two corps entered town—Howard's and Logan's—One, the diabolical 15th which Sherman has hitherto never permitted to enter a city on account of their vile and desperate character.[78] Slocum's Corps

---

77   The established pattern of careful and thorough pillage before torching continued as it had throughout the entire state of South Carolina, before and after Columbia. Both the manner of the pillage and its pattern are corroborated by many eyewitnesses, the most notable of whom is William Gilmore Simms in *Sack and Destruction*. Samuel Byers of the 5th Iowa wrote, "Plunder was the order of the day....Private residences and stores were burst open, and fired after being rifled of their most valuable contents." Charles Brown of the 21st Michigan wrote, "I saw property destroyed until I was perfectly sick of it."

78   General Oliver Otis Howard appropriated Mrs. Louisa McCord's house at the corner of Bull and Pendleton across from South Carolina College two blocks from the LeContes. Mrs. McCord hid her daughters in the upper floor. Her papers were destroyed. There are several accounts from the McCords of what transpired on that day and afterwards. General John A. Logan appropriated Colonel John S. Preston's mansion on Blanding Street. As he was leaving, his men were preparing to burn the house by setting fire to pitch barrels in the basement, but Mother Superior, Sister Baptista Lynch, who had attacked Sherman, himself a Catholic, for burning the Ursuline Convent,

remained over the river and I suppose Davis' also[79]—The devils as they marched by looked strong and well clad in dark dirty looking blue—The wagon trains were immense.

Night drew on—Of course we did not expect to sleep but we looked forward to a tolerably tranquil night. Strange as it may seem we were actually idiotic enough to believe Sherman would keep his word!—A Yankee—and Sherman! It does seem incredible, such credulity—but I suppose we were so anxious to believe him—The lying fiend! I hope retributive justice will find him out one day.—At about 7 o'clock I was standing on the back piazza on the third story. Before me the whole Southern horizon was lit up by camp fires which dotted the woods— On one side the sky was illuminated by the burning of Gen Hampton's residence[80] a few miles off in the country, on the other by some blazing buildings near the river. I had scarcely gone downstairs again when Henry told us there was a fire on Main Street—Sumter Street was brightly lighted by a burning house so near our piazza that we could feel the heat—By the red glare, we could watch the wretches walking, generally staggering, back and forth from the camp to the town— shouting, hurrahing, cursing South Carolina, screaming, blaspheming,

had a letter from him for her to take possession of any house in town. She knew that Preston's house would be especially targeted for destruction owing to its association with General Wade Hampton, so in order to spite the occupation army, she arrived on the scene with her letter. It is recorded that Logan "swore fearfully" when handed the letter. The nuns found that the soldiers had vandalized paintings and statuary, but both houses survive today.

79   General Henry W. Slocum and General Jefferson C. Davis. William Gilmore Simms noted that Sherman however did withhold Irish companies from the sacking of the city because he feared they would protect such Catholic property as St. Mary's Ursuline Convent and St. Mary's Convent School, both of which were burned after pillage and desecration of the altar, soldiers stealing its vessels after drinking wine from the Holy Chalice (*A City Laid Waste*). An excellent , lengthy memoir from a school girl present during the burning is by Sara Aldrich Richardson in *South Carolina Women in the Confederacy* (298-318).

80   "Millwood," an elegant columned brick mansion built in 1817 by General Wade Hampton I and enlarged by Wade Hampton II. In 1865, it was the principal residence of General Wade Hampton III and the seat of the Hampton family in Columbia. It sat on a 13,000 acre plantation. Wade Hampton II and III, great supporters of the turf and horse breeding, were considered the wealthiest men in America, with extensive land holdings and plantations in South Carolina, Mississippi, and Louisiana. "Millwood," complete with its race track, was situated as Emma says, in the country a few miles east of the city, and was pillaged before burning. It was set on fire in the afternoon before the city was burned later that night, as Emma accurately reports. George A. Trenholm's and Charles P. Pelham's elegant country estates east of the city and north of "Millwood" were also sought out and burned at the same time. These three structures, with their fine landscape gardens, were among the first buildings burned in the sack and destruction of the city. Some citizens of the city accurately took the smoke rising from the burning houses to be signs of what was to come for them later on that night. For a detailed account of the three country estates, see Kibler, "Columbia's Antebellum Ghost Gardens."

singing ribald songs and using such obscene language that we were forced to go indoors.[81] The fire on Main Street was now raging and we anxiously watched its progress from the upper front windows. In a little while however the flames broke forth in every direction—The drunken devils roamed about setting fire to every house the flames seemed likely to spare. They were fully equipped for the noble work they had in hand—each soldier was furnished with combustibles compactly put up—they would enter houses and in the presence of helpless women and children pour turpentine on the beds and set them on fire—Guards were rarely of any assistance—Most generally they assisted in the pillaging and firing.[82] The wretched people rushing from their burning homes were not allowed to keep even the few necessaries they gathered up in their flight—even blankets and food were taken from them and destroyed. The Firemen attempted to use their engines but the hose was cut in pieces and their lives threatened[83]—The wind blew a fearful gale wafting the flames from house to house with frightful rapidity. By midnight the whole town (except the outskirts) was wrapt in one huge blaze—Still the flames had not approached sufficiently near us to threaten our immediate safety and for some reason not a single Yankee soldier had entered our house—And now the fire instead of approaching us seemed to recede—Henry said the danger was over and sick of the dreadful scene, worn out with much fatigue and excitement, we went downstairs to our room and tried to rest—I fell into a heavy kind of stupor from which I was presently aroused by the bustle about me—Our

---

81   Simms gives an eyewitness account of the drunken, demonic revelry. In one instance, a piano was moved outside for safety and played upon by a drunken soldier. Samuel Byers of the 5th Iowa described the scene giving the name of the tune as "The Devil's Dream" played "by the light of the burning houses." One of the least profane songs reported sung by the soldiers was "Hail Columbia, fairest land! If we don't burn you, we'll be damned!"

82   Corroborated by Simms and many eyewitnesses. Simms reported that, as Emma says, in some homes beds were set on fire to initiate the houses' destruction. Simms noted that this was done after urinating on them or placing full chamber pots on them and smashed by rifle shots. Simms wrote, "parlours, articles of crockery, and even beds, were used as if they were water closets" (*Sack and Destruction,* 56). August Conrad's memoir also noted, "It was the favorite plan of the scoundrels, when they had thoroughly plundered the house, to set fire to the beds" (22). Reverend Howe of the Theological Seminary wrote, "My house was set on fire three times by the pillagers, and was put out by myself. I appealed to many officers and men for protection, but most of them laughed at me."

83   William Gilmore Simms wrote, "Engines and hose were brought out by the firemen, but these were soon driven from their labours—by the pertinacious hostility of the soldiers; their hose were hewn to pieces, and the firemen dreading worse usage to themselves, left the field in despair." (*Sack and Destruction,* 41)

neighbor Mrs Caldwell and her two younger sisters[84] stood before the fire wrapped in blankets and weeping—their home was on fire and the great sea of flame had again swept down our way, to the very campus walls[85]—I felt a kind of sickening despair and did not even stir to go and look out—After a while Jane came in to say that Aunt Josie's house was in flames—then we all went up to the front door—My God! What a scene! It was about four o'clock and the State House was one grand conflagration[86]—Imagine night turned into noonday, only with a blazing, scorching glare that was horrible—a copper coloured sky across which swept columns of black rolling smoke glittering with sparks and flying embers, while all around us were falling thickly showers of burning flakes—Everywhere the palpitating blaze, walling the streets with solid masses of flames as far as the eye could reach—filling the air with its horrible roar. On every side the crackling and devouring fire, while every instant came the crashing of timbers and the thunder of the falling buildings—A quivering molten ocean seemed to fill the air and sky—The library building opposite us seemed framed by the gushing flames & smoke, while through the windows gleamed the liquid fire— This we thought must be Aunt Josie's house. It was the next one for although hers caught frequently it was saved. The college buildings caught all along that side and had the incendiary work continued one half hour longer than it did they must have gone. All the physicians and nurses were on the roof trying to save the buildings and the poor inmates themselves such as they could crawled out while those who could not move waited to be burned to death—The common opposite the gate was crowded with homeless women & children—a few wrapped in blankets, and many shivering in the night air.[87] Such a scene as this

---

84   The sisters are identified later in the diary as Nellie and Francena.

85   The seven foot high double brick wall surrounding the campus was erected in 1835. It was credited as a chief reason the campus did not burn.

86   The Old State House, some three blocks away from the Le Conte home, was completed in 1790 from plans said to be designed by James Hoban, architect of the White House. This was the original Palladian structure in which the legislative library of 25,000 volumes and the archives were housed. The state's legislative bodies met here until it was burned in 1865. The Hall of Representatives was apparently a multi-use room that hosted, for example, exhibits of the sculpture of Hiram Powers (see Allston, *Papers of R .F. W. Allston*, 111-112), a reception for Daniel Webster, governors' inaugural balls, and Confederate bazaars. The new granite state house, still only an unroofed shell, had temporary wooden stairs and scaffolding, all burned. The plan was to explode it, but there was insufficient powder.

87   The same gatherings occurred on the grounds of the state insane asylum and Sydney Park. At the latter David Conyngham of the *New York Herald* stated that here the women were further robbed by soldiers of items they had salvaged from their burned homes as they sat

with the drunken fiendish soldiery in their dark uniforms, infuriated, cursing, screaming, exulting in their work, came nearer realizing the material ideal of hell than anything I ever expect to see again. They call themselves Sherman's "hell hounds"—

Mother collected together some bedding, clothing and food which Henry carried to the back of the garden and covered them with a hastily ripped up carpet to protect them from the sparks and flakes of fire. He worked so hard, so faithfully and tried to comfort mother as best he could while she was sobbing and crying at the thought of being left shelterless with a delicate baby. While this was going on I stood with Mary Ann at the kitchen door—She tried to speak hopefully. I could not cry—it was all too horrible—yet I felt the house must burn—By what miracle it was saved I can not think—No effort could be made—no one was on the roof which was old and dry and all the while the sparks and burning timbers were flying over it like rain. When the few things she tried to save were moved, mother took up little Carrie who was sleeping unconsciously, and wrapping ourselves in shawls and blankets we went to the front door and waited for the house to catch—There we stood, watching and listening to the roaring and crashing. It seemed inevitable—and they declared they would not leave a house standing. What would become of us? It was a fearful question. Then I thought of our beloved house. I could almost see the flames consuming it—I thought of father's library—every book of which I love. I thought of my own dear room—Oh it was dreadful. We owe our safety to the presence of Yankee wounded in the hospital. They were about to leave it to its fate when Dr. Thomson asked an officer if he would suffer his own men to be burnt up. That altered the case entirely. The officer said the hospital <u>must</u> be saved. He & some of his men came to Dr T's assistance and by desperate efforts it <u>was</u> saved. At 6 o'clock Sherman gave the signal, a blast on the bugle, for the cessation of the fire, and in 15 minutes the flames ceased spreading.[88] By 7 the last flame had expired.

---

huddled with their little piles of family portraits, blankets, bundles of clothing , and valuables. (Conyngham, 59-60). Simms added that the huddled groups had "fire balls" lobbed at them from the park's heights "and the wretched fugitives were forced to scatter." Joe Saunier of the 4th Ohio wrote, "Never in our lives have we seen such destruction and desolation. The people were in the parks and the woods and the fields without shelter."

88   Emma's account of the bugle blast is corroborated by James G. Gibbes, who wrote that two buglers entered the city in the morning and after their bugling not a dwelling was fired and the chaos stopped short (*Who Burnt Columbia?*, p. 19).

I think it was about 6 o'clock that a crowd of drunken soldiery assaulted the campus gate & threatened to overpower the guard. They swore the college buildings should <u>not</u> be spared. By great exertions Dr T. found Sherman & got a strong guard in time to secure the hospital. When there was no longer any danger we went downstairs again. Mrs C (who had been to see after her house) returned & sitting down sobbed convulsively as she told us of the insults she had received. She also said a Yankee officer riding by ordered some men to stop pillaging her house. She was so broken down and humbled by that terrible night that she turned to him & said, "Oh, Sir, please make them stop. You don't know what I have suffered this night." "I don't care a damn for your sufferings," he replied, "but my men have no right to pillage against orders." Fortunately—oh so fortunately for us the hospital is so strictly guarded that we are unmolested within its walls.

O that long twelve hours! Never surely again will I live through such a night of horrors—the memory of it will haunt me as long as I shall live!—It seemed as if the day would never come—The sun rose at last, dim and red through the thick murky atmosphere—It set last night on a beautiful town full of women and children—it shone dully down this morning on smoking ruins and abject misery. I do not know how the others felt after the strain of the fearful excitement but I seemed to sink into a dull apathy—We none seemed to have the energy to talk—After a while breakfast came in—a sort of mockery, for no one could eat. After taking a cup of coffee and bathing my face begrimed with smoke I felt better, and the memory of the night seemed like a frightful dream—I have scarcely slept for three nights yet my eyes are not heavy.

During the forenoon Aunt Josie and Aunt Jane came over to see how we had fared. We met as after a long separation and for some seconds no one could speak—then we exchanged experiences.[89] They were nearer the flames than we, but they had Dr Carter with them—someone to look to and to help them.[90] Aunt Josie says the northern side of their house became so heated that no one could remain on that side—The house caught fire three times—Being outside the hospital buildings

---

89   Josephine LeConte's letter detailing the family's experiences that night is one of the appendices of this book.
90   Carter was probably a Confederate surgeon working at the campus hospital with Dr. Thomson. He is not in the Columbia City Directory for 1860. He may have been Thomas Flournoy Carter (1828-1873), a native of Augusta, Ga.

they were more exposed than we. Once a number of Yankees rushed in saying the roof was on fire—Andrew, the negro boy, followed them up, saw them tear up the tin roofing and place lighted combustibles, and after they went down he succeeded in extinguishing them. A tolerably faithful guard was some protection to them. The view from the attic windows commanded the whole town and Aunt Jane said it was like one surging ocean of flame. She thought with us that it was more like the Medieval pictures of hell than anything she had ever imagined. We do not know the extent of the destruction but we are told that the greater por[tion] of the town is in ashes—perhaps the loveliest town in all our Southern country. This is civilized warfare! This is the way in which the "cultured" Yankee nation wars upon women and children—Failing with our men in the field, this is the way they must conquer! I suppose there was scarcely an able bodied man except the hospital physicians in the whole 20,000 people.[91] It is so easy to burn the houses over the heads of helpless women and children and then turn them with insults & sneers into the streets. One expects these people to lie and steal but it does seem such an outrage even upon degraded humanity that those who practise such wanton and useless cruelty should call themselves men. It seems to us even a contamination to look at these devils. Think of the degradation of being conquered and ruled by such a people! It seems to us now as if we would choose extermination first. I have only had to speak once to one of the blue coated fiends. I went to the front door to bid Francena & Nellie C. goodbye early this morning when a soldier came up the steps and asked me who was the mayor—"Dr. Goodwyn," I answered shortly and turned away—"Do you know his initials?" "No" and I shut the door quickly behind me.

The State House of course is burned and they talk of blowing up the new incompleted granite one, but I do not know if it can be done in its unfinished unroofed condition—We dread tonight—Mother asked Dr Thomson (who has been very kind in coming in and in keeping us posted) for a guard but he says it is unnecessary as double guards will be placed throughout the city. Dr. T. says some of the officers feel very much ashamed of last night's work—Their compunctions must have visited them since daylight. The men openly acknowledge that they

---

91   Miers noted that "Emma exaggerated." Simms, however, wrote that "the male population" consisted of only "aged men, invalids, and decrepits" (*Sack and Destruction*, 44).

received orders to burn & plunder before they crossed the river. The drunken scoundrels who tried to force their way into the campus this morning have been under guard at the gate—several hundred of them—fighting and quarrelling among themselves for two or three hours.

Poor father! What will be his state of mind when he hears of all this—the first reports that reach him will be even exaggerated. It is some comfort to us in our uncertainty & anxiety to hope that he may be safe. The explosion last night was the accidental blowing up of the Charleston freight depot. There had been powder stored there and it was scattered thickly over the floor. The poor people and negroes went in with torches to search for provisions.

When will these Yankees go! That we may breath freely again! The past three days are more like three weeks. And yet when they are gone we may be worse off—With the whole country laid waste and the railroads cut in every direction. Starvation seems to stare us in the face. Our two families have between them a few bushels of corn and a little musty flour. We have no meat but the negroes give us a little bacon every day.

8 p.m.

There has been no firing as yet. All is comparatively quiet. These buildings are surrounded by a heavy guard and we are told they are distributed throughout the city. All day the devils have been completing their work of plunder but in the hospital here we have been exempt from this. I remember how blest we have been I can not be too thankful. We have the promise of a quiet night but dare not trust our hopes—there is no telling what diabolical intentions they may have. O if they were only gone, even to the last straggler! What a load would be lifted from our hearts. We are anxious to learn the fate of our friends but the little we can gather (except from Aunt Josie and Mrs Green) is through the negroes, and ours scarcely dare venture up town. The Yankees plunder the negroes as well as the whites[92] and I think they

---

92   Simms noted, "The negroes were treated as brutally as their masters and were equally robbed of their small possessions." Again, he said, "The poor negroes were victimized by their assailants, many of them being left in a condition little short of death." David Conyngham wrote in the *New York Herald* that "Negro women were for the most part victims of the soldiers' lust. A number of them were woefully mistreated and ravished....The next morning their unclothed bodies bearing the marks of detestable crimes, were found about the city." Reverend Peter Shand's

are becoming somewhat disgusted with their <u>friends</u>. Although the servants seem quite willing, it is difficult to get any work out of them on account of the wild excitement. Ah! the dreadful excitement. I seem to stand it very well, but it seems to me we must all be ill when it is over.—Anxiety, distress, want of rest and food, must tell upon us. Mrs Wilson (Mr Shand's daughter) with a babe one week old, was moved last night from her father's burning house.[93] The Burroughs escaped with only the clothing they wore. Many many fared similarly. Some tried to save a little food—even this was torn from their hands. I have heard a number of distressing incidents but have not time to write them down. O the sorrow and misery of this unhappy town! From what I hear their chief aim while taunting helpless women has been to "humble their pride"—"Southern pride." [94]—"Where now," they would hiss—"is all your pride"—"See what we have brought you to!" "This is what you get for setting yourselves up as better than other folks."—The women acted with quiet dignity—and refused to lower themselves by any retort. Someone told me the following: Some soldiers were pillaging the house of a lady—One asked her if they had not humbled her pride <u>now</u>. "No indeed" she said "Nor can you ever." "You <u>fear</u> us anyway"—"No she said. "By G—you <u>shall</u> fear me." And he cocked his pistol and put it to her head. "Are you afraid now?" She folded her arms and looking him steadily in the eye, said contemptuously, "No." He dropped his pistol and with an exclamation of admiration left her.[95]

---

elderly maid was drowned in a puddle left by the cut fire hoses, as told in Daniel Trezevant's diary (SCL). August Conrad also tells of himself witnessing the violence against women, acts that particularly outraged him.

93   Joseph LeConte identifies the Rev. Dr. Robert Wilson as rector of St. Luke's Episcopal Church in Charleston, "at this time in Columbia with his father-in-law," Rev. Shand (*'Ware Sherman*, 138). Reverend Peter J. Shand was minister of Trinity Episcopal Church from 1834 to 1886. Simms recorded that Shand "sought in vain to save a trunk containing the sacred vessels of his church. It was violently wrested from his keeping, and his struggle to save it only provoked rougher usage." (*Sack and Destruction*, 62). Shand himself gave the account: "The communion plate, a valuable set, was forcibly taken from the Rector by a band of soldiers, as he was endeavouring to carry it from his burning house. It has never been recovered." (C. C. Pinckney, *Report of the Committee on the Destruction of Churches*, 14)

94   Perhaps Emma had heard some such comment as Sherman's promise "to bring proud Southern women to the washtub."

95   Simms wrote similarly: "To inspire terror in women, strange to say, seemed to them a sort of heroism…but the women of Columbia behaved themselves nobly under their insults. They preserved that patient, calm demeanour, that simple firmness, which so becomes humanity in the hour of trial, when nothing can be opposed to the tempest but the virtue of inflexible endurance." He added that the bravery and spirit of our women were "especially a subject of acknowledgement" among the soldiers (*Sack and Destruction*).

Sunday Feb. 19th

The day has passed quietly as regards the Yankees. About eleven o'clock last night as everything seemed quiet and Henry intended to sit up, I thought I would follow mother's example and try to get some rest. So without taking off my clothes—only loosening them—I lay down and slept soundly all night. I woke at seven much refreshed—Sallie in a few moments opened her eyes and said "O mother is it already day? I am so glad—I thought the light in the window was the reflection from a fire."

I rose took off my clothes for the first time in three days, and after bathing and putting on clean clothes I felt like another being.

This morning fresh trouble awaited us.—We thought the negroes were going to leave us. While we were on the back piazza Mary Ann came to us weeping and saying she fears the Yankees were going to force Henry to go off with them and of course she would have to go with her husband. He did not want to go and would not she said unless forced. She seemed greatly distressed at the thought of leaving the master and mistress who had supplied the place of father and mother to her, an orphan. The others, Maria & her children, want to go I think. They have been dressed in their Sundays best all day. Mary Ann when she came to get dinner, said she could cook two more meals for us anyway. Mother went over to Aunt Josie's to consult her—She advised that if they left, mother should get Dr. T. to put some sick men in our house to protect it and we must all move over there as they have two white servants. On her return however she talked to Henry, who vows he will never leave us unless dragged away, and he thinks he can avoid them. They are free, however, at present, and we ask as little as possible of them— such as cooking our little food and bringing water from the well—The water works being destroyed we have to get water from the campus well.[96] If Jane offers to clean up our room—all very well—if not, we do it ourselves. This afternoon I washed the dinner things and put the room to rights. The house is untouched except this one room we live in, which I manage to keep neat & clean. This is my first experience in work of this kind and I find it is better than doing nothing. The negroes when

---

96   The water works were created in the 1850s to bring piped water to the city. The gardens of Louisa McCord and John S. Preston were thus able to have ornamental fountains in their gardens.

we ask, however, seem quite willing and have given us not the slightest impertinence.

While mother was at Aunt Josie's, Sallie and I took Carrie up in the drawing room to amuse her.—While we stood by the front window the house was shaken by a terrible explosion. As the gas works were burning at the time I concluded it was the gasometer but remembering we had no gas for two or three days that seemed impossible. Henry has just explained it. Our men had buried a number of shells near the river. In trying to excavate them one went off accidentally and exploded the rest, killing and wounding a great many Yankees. How I rejoice to think of any of them being killed. Mr Bell[97] says (he occupies the Barnwells' house) about 200 were burnt up Friday night, drunk perhaps.[98] If only the whole army could have been roasted alive.

The provost guard is encamped opposite the campus—It consists of one battalion and is to remain until the last straggler leaves the town. Two of its officers went to Aunt Josie's and saying they wished quarters opposite their camp, she was obliged to accommodate them and give up her library for their use. Their horrid old gridiron of a flag is flaunting its bars in our faces all day. Ever since dark, thick clouds of smoke have been rolling up from the arsenal and I fear the flames will spread over the hill. Mary Ann came to us in great distress this afternoon to tell us that a Yankee had sworn to her that these buildings should be

---

97   Unidentified. Edwin Scott wrote that the Bell family of Granby were part of "a circle of refined society that was at once moral and elevated" (*Random Recollections of a Long Life*, 112.)
98   In one of many attempts to deconstruct Emma's diary, Miers notes that Emma's "report was fictitious." Samuel Byers of the 5th Iowa, however, records, "Numbers of intoxicated soldiers revelled in burning houses until the charred walls fell in, when they perished beneath them." Hanoverian Consul August Conrad wrote that he saw "drunken soldiers rushing from house to house, emptying them of their valuables and firing them…officers and men reveling on the wines until the burning houses buried them in their drunken orgies." Simms wrote: "No less than 150 of the drunken creatures perished miserably among the flames kindled by their own comrades… Sherman's officers themselves are reported to have said that they lost more men in the sack and burning of the city …than in all their fights while approaching it." Simms continued, "It is also suggested that the orders which Sherman issued at daylight on Saturday morning for the arrest of the fire, were issued in consequence of the loss of men" (*Sack and Destruction*, 43). U. S. General O. O. Howard himself wrote that "hundreds" of soldiers were killed in the fire (*Autobiography of Oliver Otis Howard*, 122). Perhaps the most grisly account of burned U.S. soldiers was given by Josie LeConte in a letter of 28 February 1865. Here she described frantic screaming drunken soldiers crying for help and burned to death in a building's upper floor, while being cheered by U. S. soldiers who thought they were Confederates. After the building collapsed, U. S. soldiers "severed the heads from the bodies, caught them up on their bayonets, and danced around to the tune of 'damnation to the rebels,' little knowing they were their own men" (as quoted in Culpepper, *Women of the Civil War South*, p. 70).

burned tonight. Enquiring of an officer mother was assured there was no danger—I suppose it was only a drunken threat. Mother looked over the town this morning from Aunt Josie's attic window. She describes a scene of fearful desolation. Here all is hidden from us—When they are gone I will walk out of the campus & see it all—Yet how I dread it! Poor Columbia! Sometimes I try to picture it to myself as it now is—but I can not. I always see the leafy streets and lovely gardens, the familiar houses. I can not imagine the ruins and ashes to save my life. <u>How</u> I <u>hate</u> the people who have done this!

A few moments ago there was a violent ring at the bell. I was the only person awake and I roused Jane up and sent her upstairs. It was some Yankee officer who wished to know where Mayor Goodwyn lives. Sherman it seems wishes to appoint a meeting with him in order to leave arms for the citizens to protect themselves from stragglers.[99]

Monday Feb. 20th

Quite early this morning a Yankee entered the yard looking for Henry, who forthwith locked himself in his room. Mother went out and asked the mean filthy devil if he wished to make Henry go against his will. He hesitated a little and said "No," but he wished to see him. The soldier—the dirtiest, meanest looking creature imaginable—told mother, when she threatened to send for the guard if he did not leave, that he was one of the guard himself. "Well" said mother, "there are two officers at my sister's house and I will send to them." The Yankee turned and left the yard. Mrs Bell tells me that Sherman turned loose upon us a brigade that he had never allowed to enter any other city on account of their desperate and villainous character. And yet they talk now of being ashamed of what followed and try to lay it on the whiskey they found.

Shortly after breakfast (oh! joyful sight) the two corps encamped behind the campus back of us marched by with all their immense wagon trains on their way from Columbia. They tell us all will be gone by tomorrow evening. O that we were completely rid of them and that father were with us again! I might then know what it is to feel happy one moment—Under other circumstances it would have been a wonderful

---

99   Simms reports it this way: "So he [Sherman] left with the people of Columbia a hundred old Columbia muskets for their protection, while emptying their arsenals of a choice collection of beautiful Enfield rifles" (*Sack and Destruction*, 86).

sight to see this great army with its endless train march by[100]—With the memory of Friday night burned in, it was hard to look at them.

A great drove of lean ill looking cattle was driven into the campus today—our two cows have not been taken from us.

Neither the Roman Catholic or Episcopal (Trinity) or Presbyterian churches were burnt.[101] It was a miracle the latter was saved—everything around it was destroyed. In Trinity churchyard soldiers were encamped. Of course there was no service in any of the churches yesterday—no church bells ringing—the Yankees riding up & down the streets—the provost guard at work putting up their camp—there was nothing to suggest Sunday.

What balmy delicious weather we have had for three days past— Most fortunate it is or there would have been more suffering. Henry has already cut down two trees in the yard to give us wood.

Mother has just this moment returned from Aunt Josie's bringing the news that the last of the army is leaving the city. The provost guard has broken up camp also. This leaves the terror of stragglers before us— We expected the guard would remain a day or two. There is no knowing what outrages may be committed. Mother is going to try to get Dr Thomson[102] to stay here at night—She wants to send me to Aunt Josie's but I will not leave her alone.—We must trust to Henry's protection.

Tuesday [Feb.] 21st

The night with its fear of stragglers is past and we may breathe more freely but not less sadly—The destruction and desolation around us which we could not feel while under such excitement and fear now exerts its full sway. Sad? The very air is fraught with sadness and

---

100   August Conrad's memoir explained that it required "an entire train of transport wagons" to carry gold, silver, and precious items of value (27). Like Emma, he described their train of wagons as "endless" (31).

101   The burned churches and church properties included Christ Episcopal, the Lutheran and Methodist churches, the old Baptist church, the Presbyterian Reading Rooms, Trinity's "picturesque" Rectory, Trinity's Lecture Rooms and Sunday School House and parish records, the Ursuline Convent, its four pastoral residences, St. Mary's (Catholic) College, and Columbia's Synagogue. The loss of Christ Church, which had a seating capacity of 600, was deemed by the Diocese to be the greatest Episcopal loss in the state because newly constructed in 1859 and the second largest Episcopal church outside Charleston. The church contents included a new organ, library, and expensive furnishings (C. C. Pinckney, *Report of the Committee on the Destruction of Churches*, 14).

102   See note 64.

silence. The few noises that break the stillness seem melancholy and the sun does not seem to shine as brightly—seeming to be dimmed by the sight of so much misery. I was at Aunt Josie's this morning and there learned for the first time the extent of suffering. O God! When we think of what we have escaped and how almost miraculously we have been saved, we should never rise from our knees! There is not a house I believe in Columbia that was not pillaged—Those that the flames spared were entered by brutal soldier[s] and everything wantonly destroyed.[103] The men supplied with combustibles set fire to the houses—pouring oil over the beds—turpentine, etc—When the fire companies at first tried to work they cut the hose & would not allow any effort to put out the fire[104]—the streets were filled with terrified women and children who were offered every insult and indignity short of personal outrage—they were allowed to save nothing but what clothes they wore and there is now great suffering for food. It would be impossible to describe or even conceive the pandemonium and horror. There is no shadow of doubt that the town was burned by Sherman's order. All through Georgia, it is said, he promised his men full license in South Carolina—The signals both for firing & ceasing were given—the soldiers were provided with the materials for the work. And yet I hear he already denies it and tries to put the responsibility on Gen Hampton.

At one time last Friday night when Aunt Josie's house and other buildings near were taking fire, the college buildings were given up and the poor wounded soldiers who could not be moved resigned themselves to death. Dr Carter[105] says it was a touching sight to see the poor fellows trying manfully to nerve themselves to meet their fate. And there was the regiment ostensibly sent to extinguish the fire, calmly looking on without raising a finger, and the patrols on the streets themselves applying the torch. The hospital was saved by one Yankee Captain & two men—Yet it contained many of their own wounded soldiers. The unfinished granite

---

103   Simms corroborates Emma's description: The guards of "many houses" helped the soldiers in destroying and smashing. David Conyngham, reporter for the *New York Herald,* wrote that "A troop of cavalry patrolled the streets, but I did not once see them interfering with the groups that rushed about to fire and pillage the houses." August Conrad also corroborated the destructive activity of the lower officers.

104   Corroborated by Simms.

105   Joseph LeConte described the evacuation of the sick and wounded from the campus hospital. The men dragged themselves onto the college green's center. He noted that "more of twenty of them died the next day in consequence of exposure and fright" (*'Ware Sherman,* 141-142).

State house was not blown up because they were short of powder and it is unroofed. All that could be destroyed was ruined by the burning of the work sheds—fine carving, capitals, columns—ornamental work, etc.[106] I can hardly help feeling that our total exemption from insult and plunder was in some way due to the influence of the strange man who called himself Davis and promised us protection. Why in many houses the very guards stationed to protect helped the soldiers in smashing and destroying. It is sickening to listen to the tales of distress, much more to try to write of it—A heavy curse has fallen on this town— From a beautiful bustling city, it is turned into a desert. Henry has just come in from uptown. He gave us a description of what he saw. "O Miss" he said "it is dreadful, dreadful—I lost my way and wouldn't have known where I was but for the State house."

How isolated and dreary we feel. How completely cut off from the world! No longer the shrill whistle of the engine—no daily mail—the morning brings no paper with news from the outside—no lights—no going to & fro—It is as if a city in the midst of business and activity were suddenly smitten with some appalling curse. One feels awed if by chance the dreary stillness is broken by a laugh or too loud a voice. How unhappy poor father & Uncle John—Julian and Cousin Johnny will be when they hear of this!—there has even been a report afloat that Aunt Josie's house was burned & that Cousin Lula perished in the flames—if they should hear that!

I wonder if the vengeance of heaven will not pursue such fiends! Before they came here I thought I hated them as much as was possible— Now I know there are no limits to the feeling of hatred.

Wed. Feb. 22nd

I meant last night to write down some description of what I had seen but I was too wretchedly depressed and miserable to even think of it.—This morning we have heard that he is safe and I can take up my journal again—Yesterday afternoon we walked all over the town in company with Miss Ellen LaBorde[107]—Yes, I have seen it all—I have

---

106   Photographs of the heaped marble on the State House grounds prove Emma's accuracy. Simms noted that the workers' sheds and the architect's offices were also burned.
107   Ellen Carroll LaBorde (1832-1902) was one of South Carolina College Professor Maximilian LaBorde's daughters.

seen the "Abomination of Desolation."—It is even worse than I thought. The place is literally in ruins. The entire heart of the city is in ashes—only the outer edges remain. On the whole length of Sumter St not one house beyond the first block after the campus is standing except the brick house of Mr. Mordecai—Standing in the centre of the town as far as the eye can reach nothing is to be seen but heaps of rubbish, tall dreary chimneys and shattered brick walls, while

"In the hollow windows dreary

Horror's sitting."[108]

Poor old Columbia—where is all her beauty—So admired by strangers, so loved by her children!—She can only excite the pity of the former and the tears of the latter. I hear several Yankee officers remarked to some citizens on the loveliness of their town as they first saw it by sunrise across the river.—Blanding St crossing Main & Sumter at right angles the finest street in town is also a sad picture. The Preston house with its whole square of beautiful gardens escaped—it was Gen Logan's headquarters. The Crawford house, the Bryce's, the Howe's and one or two others also escaped. All nearer Main St were burned. The Clarkson house is a heap of brick with most of its tall columns standing, blackened by the smoke—Bedells lovely little house is in ruins while as if in mockery the shrubbery is not even scorched.[109]—But I can not particularize—with <u>very</u> few exceptions, all our friends are homeless. We enter Main St—the long business street—Since the war in crowd and bustle it has rivaled a city thoroughfare—What desolation! Everything has vanished as by enchantment—Stores merchants customers—all the eager faces gone.—Only three or four dismal looking people to be seen cautiously picking their way over heaps of brick and

---

108   These are lines from Schiller's "The Song of the Bell."

109   Emma was correct in every instance. The John S. Preston mansion was General John A. Logan's headquarters, saved from firing by Sister Baptista Lynch (see note 75). The John A. Crawford house still stands at the corner of Bull and Blanding. It is said that Crawford, an Irish immigrant, tried to save his favorite horse by taking it upstairs. Dr. George Howe's house was owned by the clergyman friend of Reverend Dr. Palmer, and a professor at the Presbyterian Seminary on Blanding Street nearby, now the Robert Mills Ainsley Hall Mansion, also a survivor of the burning. The Thomas B. Clarkson house, the finest mansion ever built in the city, constructed by Senator and Gov. James Henry Hammond in 1839, was the city's greatest loss of domestic architecture. A photograph of the tall columns that surrounded the structure shows Emma's description to be accurate. An eyewitness of the burning describes the flames seen through the columns as they devoured the structure. Bedell's house was C. A. Bedell's home described as burned in Simms, 79.

timber—The wind moans among the bleak chimneys and whistles through the gaping windows of some hotel or warehouse. The market a ruined shell supported by crumbling arches—its spire fallen in and with it the old town clock whose familiar stroke we miss so much. After trying to distinguish localities and hunting for familiar buildings we turned to Arsenal Hill. Here things looked more natural—The Arsenal was destroyed but comparatively few dwellings—Also the park and its surroundings looked familiar[110]—As we passed the old State House going back, I paused to gaze on the ruins—only the foundations and chimneys recall the brilliant scene enacted there one short month ago. And I compared that scene with its beauty, gayety and festivity, the halls so elaborately decorated, the surging throng—with this. I reached home sad at heart and full of all I had seen. Presently we heard a commotion in the yard. Running out on the back verandah, we saw standing in the middle of the yard, Sandy and the boys and the negroes who had remained grouped around them. As soon as they saw us Annie screamed: "The Yankees had caught 'em. Mass Johnny's come back and Master's took prisoner!" Asking Sandy about father, he said that he and Capt Green were in the woods when the party was captured. We could learn nothing succinct from him and all tired as we were, rushed over to see Johnny. We found him in the kitchen with Cousin Lula and two white servants—All the rest were out. Johnny gave us a description of their capture. The Yankees they fell in with treated them kindly and he thought Uncle John would be paroled. He thought father must have been captured as the woods were alive with Yankees—he did not see how he could escape—and he feared he would fare worse for being caught trying to escape—And even if he did escape, the country had been so entirely swept that he could get nothing to eat. Father and Capt G were out scouting when the negroes were taken. As Johnny started home yesterday and had seen father last on Sunday morning there seemed little ground to hope that he had not been taken. Yet if I had been certain of his capture it would have been less dreadful than the

---

110   Sidney Park. As Emma reports, Arsenal Hill with its several mansions was not burned. Today, it is the site of South Carolina's Governor's Mansion, reclaimed from the officer's quarters of the Arsenal Hill Military Academy, and several elegant restored antebellum mansions. This is the site of many of the dances Emma says she attended after the war. To get there, she said she had to cross a mile of ruins. Arsenal Hill was on the opposite side of the city from the campus. The prominent chimneys in the central city caused the townspeople to nickname burned Columbia "Chimneyville." (See the Adger Autograph Album, Historic Columbia Collection).

thought of his hiding in the woods, cold, hungry, and the possibility of being shot—It was dreadful—Everything was burst open—all our silver & valuable stolen—articles of clothing slashed up by bayonets[111] and burned with father's valuable books carried off for safety. And all our table linen and bedding, blankets etc—But we did not once think of these things in the great anxiety and distress about father. Then Aunt Josie, Aunt Jane, Mrs. Green and Cousin Ada came in. Cousin Lula went to break the news—Aunt Josie was quite overcome—She and mother wept together—Aunt Jane trying to comfort them.

I drew back in the shadow of the staircase—it seemed as if my heart would break, and I cried by myself till Cousin Ada turning said "Poor Emma" and put her arms around me. It was dark and we had to go home—I rushed upstairs to my room and threw myself down beside the bed—My heart was bursting—one horrible picture always before my eyes—

This morning mother learned from Moultrie Gibbes[112] that father is safe—He saw him at a house 18 miles from Columbia—It is impossible to tell of the relief after such suspense. I feel so thankful.—We learned from Sandy that the negroes at the Nitre plantation, who were along, have taken possession of and brought home some of our things. Mother & Aunt Josie went to Capt Stanley of the provost guard and he has promised to institute a thorough search for them. How unfortunate that we should have sent off our valuables! But how could we guess our house would not be treated like the rest. Luckily we did not send off our summer clothing. Sandy says they dived immediately into the box of mine and told him to tell his mistress they were much obliged, as they swallowed hock and champagne.—

---

111 The bayonet slashing of property, especially portraits and other art work, was a common practice. The various paintings in the extensive art collection of Dr. Robert W. Gibbes were "with their swords slashed across—not out of their frames to carry away, but zig zag across –with the sole object of destruction" (Cole Blease, as quoted in Alexander Moore, ed. Robert W. Gibbes, *A Memoir of James Deveaux*, xxxi). Nell Graydon records that Mrs. Fair was "prevented from taking a portrait of her mother from her burning home." A soldier "snatched the portrait and cut it to bits with his sabre" (139). Editor James Kibler has an oversized portfolio of Rubens engravings, each of whose pages has a zig zag slash from top to bottom occasioned by soldiers of Kilpatrick's Cavalry in their looting of Pomaria Plantation some 25 miles northwest of Columbia. Pomaria's framed portrait of Rubens' Madonna and Child was also slashed.
112 This was William Moultrie Gibbes (1839-1921). Joseph identified him as the son of Dr. Robert W. Gibbes. He was a cadet of the Military Academy in Columbia, then stationed at Pocotaligo, S.C. (*'Ware Sherman*, 4, 117).

Henry says one mill has been spared and we can get corn ground. The negroes are flocking in from the devastated country to be fed. Mayor Goodwyn has ordered them to be sent back as the town is threatened with starvation. Indeed I do not know what will become of us unless relief comes in from Edgefield or Augusta—In every other direction we understand the country is a desert—Orangeburg, Winnsboro, Chester, Camden, all in ashes. Incarnate fiends! And Sherman!

"O for a tongue to curse the slave!"[113]

February 23rd

The days are now as monotonous as possible—I do not leave the house. Yesterday, except the portion spent in writing this record, was passed wandering aimlessly about the house or sitting listless in the sun—This morning I felt I must not be so idle. I tried to read a volume of Mad. de Stael "De la Litterature"[114]—it was impossible—I tried something lighter, one of Dickens—I soon found I did not know what I was reading. I thought of commencing a pair of gloves I have been meaning to make for father—the very thought seemed to make me weary. I suppose it is the reaction from the frightful strain and nervous tension—the violent excitement. And then the uncertainty of the future—What is to become of us. If father would only come home— if we could only leave this desolate place. Sometimes I feel a restless impatience to know what is going on in the world from which we are cut off. And then I feel at times an entire and apathetic indifference as to what should transpire.

Mother saw Mr Gibbes[115] yesterday herself. He says he was passing a house and hearing some Confederate officers were within he desired to see them. Whereupon father & Capt Green made their appearance at the door, the former with a cup of coffee in his hand. At that time he was expecting to make his way to Winnsboro, but Mr G. told him the Yankees were gone in that direction and advised him to remain where he was until he heard from Columbia. I looked for him last night and

---

113   A line from Thomas Moore's 1817 poem "Lalla Rookh." The "slave" referred to is a traitor or one subservient to evildoers (meaning Yankees).
114   Madame de Stael (1766-1817), a French-Swiss author, and popular radical politicist.
115   James Guignard Gibbes, son of Dr. Robert W. Gibbes, had a government warehouse burned by Sherman. He later became mayor of Columbia.

sometimes I fear he may have been caught by Kilpatrick's raiders, but I think I have no reasonable ground for such a fear. There is nothing to do but try to be patient—Patience! How the heavy days creep by! O to see my own dear father again after all that has been gone through and suffered since we parted!

* * *

Dr Carter left for Augusta this morning and we sent letters by him to Georgia—I wrote a few pages to Cousin Ella[116]—would have written to Cousin Annie[117] but do not know where she is.—Mother wrote to Grandmother—I hope the letters will be legible enough when they reach their destination to relieve anxiety. There is not one drop of ink in the house and for ten days I have written this diary in pencil—I wish I could get letters.

Sallie has commenced studying and will recite her lessons to me tomorrow. I can not summon energy or interest to go back to my own studies. That must not be until anxiety banished we are reunited and settled down in quiet—When will that be! The Yankees talk very strongly of conquering the South immediately—if so our day of rest is far off. Somehow I am still as confident as I ever was, if only our people will be steadfast. The more we suffer, the more we should be willing to undergo rather than submit—Somehow I can not feel we can be conquered—We have lost everything—but if everything—negroes, property—all could be given back a hundredfold I would not be willing to go back to them[118]—I would rather endure any poverty than live under Yankee rule. I would rather have France or any other country for a mistress. Anything but live as one nation with <u>Yankees</u>—that word in my mind is a synonym with <u>all</u> that is <u>mean</u> despicable and abhorrent.

I hope relief will come before famine actually threatens. We have to cut our rations as short as possible to try to make the food hold out till succor comes. Father left us with some mouldy spoiled flour that was turned over to him by the Bureau—we can only possibly eat it made into batter cakes and then it is horrid—We draw rations from the town every

---

116   Emma's cousin Ella Florine Stevens (1845-1914), daughter of Joseph's sister Anne Le Conte Stevens, Emma's Aunt Annie (1825-1866).
117   Anne LeConte Anderson (1836-1922), daughter of Joseph's eldest brother William and wife Sarah, Emma's Aunt Sallie.
118   "Them" meaning the Union.

day—a tiny bit of rancid salt pork and a pint of meal. We have the batter cakes for breakfast—the bit of meat and cornbread for dinner—no supper. We fare better than some because we have the cows[119]—Mother had peas to feed them and sometimes we take a few from them to vary our diet. Today as a <u>great</u> <u>treat</u> mother gave us boiled <u>rice</u> for dinner— Some the negroes brought us in the pillage of the stores. We enjoyed it immensely—the first I have tasted in many days.[120]

February 26th Sunday

[Emma wrote Tuesday night Feb. 26th]

At last I have something joyful to chronicle. <u>Father is returned!</u> Friday evening as we all sat in the library there was a knocking at the door, then a violent ring at the bell. We knew what it meant. I rushed to the door first and opened it to fall into father's arms. What a scene! Embraces, kisses weeping—He was wet through and in rags—We hurried him to the fire and listened to the story of his escape—an escape that seemed little short of miraculous. (Here follows an account of father's and Capt G.'s adventures which I omit, as given fully in his own diary of that eventful time)[121] I am so thankful and happy every moment that I remember he is safe at home. Father describes Sherman's track up there as the same it was in the lower part of the State—Desolation and ruin. Every night the entire horizon was illuminated by burning houses. Poor Carolina! And the burning of Columbia was the most diabolical act of all the barbarous war. Father grits his teeth every time he sees the ruins or speaks of the horrors of that night.

---

119   Miers noted that Sherman left the city 500 over-aged and underfed cattle "dying of exhaustion" at the rate of 15 or 20 a day. More perceptively, Simms wrote that Sherman left "a few hundred starving cattle, of which he had robbed the starving people of Beaufort, Barnwell, Orangeburg and Lexington…Even Gen. Sherman could give to parties whom he knew, the flour and bacon which he had stolen from thousands of starving widows and orphans…The cunning of this ostentatious charity" tries "to persuade the world that the incendiarism which destroys all in its path is unpremeditated and purely accidental" (*Sack and Destruction*, 86-87). Cecelia Lawton in her reminiscences of the war in Georgia, recorded animals shot in piles after they were stolen and then deemed burdensome (*Incidents in the Life of Cecilia Lawton*). In her memoir, Emma tells the story of her mother's cows, Hook and Crook, whose excess milk she sold to the occupation garrison for money on which to live.
120   As for rice planters, as for South Carolinians in general, the Le Contes must have indeed found rice to be a treat after so many days without it. Rice was a staple of the diet surpassing corn in its manifold forms. Carolinians vowed that a day without rice is no day at all.
121   Joseph's account was published as '*Ware Sherman*.

As far as I can see the people are undemoralized and more determined than ever. The Yankee officers while here paid the tribute to the women of this state of say [*sic*] they were the most firm, obstinate and ultra rebel set of women they had encountered—If the men only prove equally so![122]

Father and I went to church this morning—We had a mournful looking congregation. Dr Howe[123] officiated, reading the first chapter of Lamentations.[124] After church we stopped at Aunt Josie's, who kindly lent us some table silver. All mother saved was three forks, 2 tablespoons and 2 teaspoons which she kept out for our use.

Today is father's birthday.

Tuesday Feb 28th

I am now fairly launched as a school ma-am. I fancy I get on pretty well considering my lack of experience. I teach Sallie arithmetic, Latin, spelling and elementary Natural Philosophy besides reading & composition. I will begin study myself when father returns from a trip down the river with Capt Green to get provisions for the town in general and our two families in particular. They propose starting tomorrow.

Cousin Ada & I went to call on Mrs C—[125] yesterday but she is not in town having run away just before the advent of the Yankees. It is not far from her house to the cemetery so we went there to look at little Josie's grave.[126] Coming home we walked down Main St—slowly in the

---

122   See note 91.

123   Dr. George Howe of the Presbyterian Theological Seminary, and an assistant to the Reverend Dr. Palmer of the First Presbyterian Church. Emma records in her memoirs that Dr. Palmer took Mrs. Howe to Savannah (41).

124   The Old Testament Book of Lamentations bewails the destruction and looting of the city of Jerusalem in 586 B.C. by the Babylonians.

125   The WPA version inserted Carroll after C—. Elizabeth Anciaux Berrien Carroll (1818-1894) was the wife of James Parsons Carroll (1809-1883). Emma wrote in her memoir that in 1865 the Carrolls had moved to Columbia from Edgefield: "Chancellor Carroll's wife was a daughter of Judge Berrien of Savannah—a distant cousin of father's –Judge Berrien's grandmother was one of the famous Eaton sisters and the sister of father's great grand-mother Valeria Eaton LeConte. Mrs. Carroll always claimed the relationship and called us cousin" (51). The cousinage included Mary Parsons Carroll Screven (1818-1894), Lillah (Eliza Anciaux Carroll, 1843-1910), and Sophie (Sophia Parsons Carroll, 1846-1923).

126   Emma's sister Eloise Josephine (1859-1861). In 1901, in his autobiography, Joseph wrote a touching account of his third child: "I cannot even mention her name without the tenderest emotions. She was the most beautiful child we ever had, with that rare combination of flaxen hair and dark eyes. Alas! We lost her just two years later. The light, the sunlight, the spiritual light seemed to have gone out of my house. Is it possible that the origin of such love can be other than immortal?"

middle of the street for fear of falling walls—trying to conjure up the well known shops & buildings from the shapeless heaps. At the Market Place we saw the old bell—"Secessia," that had rung out every state as it seceded, lying half buried in the earth and reminding me of Retzsch's last Outline in "The Song of the Bell" showing

"That all things earthly disappear."[127]

We walked through the State House yard and examined the marks of the shells on the new Capitol. Large pieces of granite are sometimes broken off—On one end alone we counted places where eight shells had struck and exploded. The terrible explosion that alarmed us so much on that terrible Friday morning of the burning, we have since learned was the accidental blowing up of the Charleston freight depot. A large quantity of provisions were stored there-in and also much powder in bags, which having broken had become scattered over the floor. Large numbers of poor people and negroes went in with <u>torches</u> to get the provision—It is said 150 or 200 people were killed.

Wed. March 1st

The first day of Spring!—A gloomy opening of the bright season—It is not cold, but dark and rainy. Father has been obliged to defer his trip on account of the weather and is waiting for a fair day. There was a rumour afloat yesterday that a negro regiment was marching from Branchville to garrison Columbia. Heavens! Have we not suffered enough? I do not believe it but the very thought is enough to make me shudder—If father succeeds in laying in a supply of food, we will probably remain here, unless father is ordered away. Communication will soon be opened with Augusta & other towns and probably with Col. St. John. As long as we stay here we have the comforts of home and are among friends. Then if the government works are moved back, I might get some kind of employment.[128]

---

127   The "Outline" refers to a book of engravings by German artist Moritz Retzsch illustrating Friedrich Schiller's poem "The Song of the Bell."
128   Emma probably means work at the Confederate government printing offices in Columbia, which employed women (the "Treasury Girls") in the printing of paper currency.

March 2nd

It still continues damp & cloudy with no immediate prospect of a favourable change.

I have not gone back to study but feel heartily ashamed of myself for not doing so—I have resolved not to be idle any longer but to go back to my books and take up again some solid reading I had planned before all this excitement.

This afternoon father called me downstairs to help him re-arrange the books. They had been packed in boxes, before the Yankees came, for removal but father finding it impossible to take them off, judged they would be safer in the cases as the soldiers would tumble them out in search of valuables, so just before he left he had Henry put them back—of course he replaced them pell mell without any regard to order.

I had a good laugh with Sallie—I mentioned in my account of the shelling of the town on Thursday that the man Davis brought me a box of feathers. I had laid them away and did not think of them till today when I came across them and we were looking over them, selecting some that I thought would make a pretty fan. Near the bottom of the box Sallie spied a folded paper—A leaf torn from a notebook. She opened it. At the top of the page was a rude drawing of two hearts—this the note said—"portrayed two hearts surrounded by rosebuds" (the rosebuds been [*sic*] entirely imaginary) "May they (continued the note) prove an emblem of our hearts. May they be joined by the golden links of friendship and may the rosebuds of life entwine them. And though many hundred miles separate us may we always be firm friends."—Well if that individual is not a queer fish, I never met one. He was a pretty rough specimen, but if we owe anything to his kindness of heart, I ought not to be too hard on his coarseness. Of course Sallie got a lot of fun out of it showing it in high glee to father who was greatly amused over it. The fellow had a wonderfully keen insight into character. The evening he talked with me after father was gone he hit off his character except in one or two points wonderfully, considering how absolutely different he was. He read both mother's and my characters too—Mine, except for the flattery he threw in, was very correct too.

March 7th Tuesday

Last Friday (3rd) we received two pieces of good news. In the first place Dr Pratt arrived with four wagons for our relief. Two hours after receiving father's letter he started—In that short time provisions were hastily collected and clothing for father, uncle John & Capt G. (father has been wearing a pair of blue trousers taken from a dead Yankee soldier at the hospital and given him by one of the doctors). The officers of the Nitre Bureau contributed—throwing in shirts, collars, socks etc etc—When he got to Prof Holmes' in Edgefield,[129] that generous hearted friend set to work and loaded up a wagon with bacon, corn, clothing, etc. and sent word we must all come to his house right away. Such friends in times of like these [sic] of scarcity & selfishness are indeed to be appreciated. Dr Pratt left so hurriedly that he did not even go home to bid his wife goodbye—only despatched her a note. He says no one in Augusta has the slightest conception of the desolation here. They suppose that only Main Street was burned, and that, the Yankees said, was done accidentally by our <u>own</u> troops in destroying cotton(!)[130] As soon as the state of things was better understood, contributions poured in. Our necessities are supplied for the present and we need not now draw rations from the town as we have been doing ever since the fire. The mayor issues rations to 7000 people—All that is left of a population of about 30,000. The original population of 12,000 was enormously increased since the war by refugees and other sources.

The other piece of good news was received that night, viz: that Uncle John was paroled in Chester. Aunt Josie's joy was unbounded and her excitement brought on a severe attack of palpitation of the heart—Last evening she received a letter from him—He is within 27 miles of Columbia but is waiting to get a conveyance—One of his feet is so sore from making a march of 50 miles with the Yankees that he can not walk it. Chester was not burned—the Yankees did not go either there or to Yorkville. The greater part of Winnsboro was destroyed and the whole of Lexington—in fact every town & village in their track. Dr Pratt stayed with us while here.

---

129   Professor E. S. Holmes, superintendent of Nitre and Mining Districts No. 6, S. C. He was in Augusta when he aided Joseph to return to Columbia.
130   General Sherman falsely accused the Confederate forces of deliberately setting fire to bales of cotton in Main Street just before they evacuated from the city, thus putting the blame on them for the burning of Columbia. He later said he lied on purpose to shake the state's love of General Wade Hampton.

Father, giving up his expedition down the river, returned with him to Augusta yesterday the 6th to see what he could do about getting supplies from there. We expect him back in one or two days.

We can hear nothing from our army. For the first time we are without the excitement of daily telegraphic news and miss the breakfast table discussion of the war news, and the movements of the forces. We live in absolute ignorance while our fate is being decided—and speedy peace, and long continued war are trembling in the balance. At all events we miss perhaps a thousand unfounded & conflicting rumours. We are hoping for intervention, but that may mean humiliating concessions. If recognition means the opening of our ports only that would be all we would ask. Once freely supplied with materials for war we would soon be independent. That is all we need.

Wednesday March 8th

Uncle John got home last night. It has been raining all day and I have not been to see him. He is confined to the house with his foot.

I am back at my books again and read a great deal. I do nothing else—except of course knitting which does not interfere at all with my reading. I have gone at old Gibbon again and mean to finish him.[131] Am also reading Hitchcock—especially in the metaphysical portions of the latter.[132] I need father so much. I hope he will not have to go off again—I do want to get steadily and systematically at work once more.

Friday March 10th

Today is the day of Fasting and prayer appointed by the president. It rained so hard all the morning however that none of us went to church. Even if the weather were favourable, I could not go as I am not at all well—nor have been for several days but only began to feel like giving up yesterday. Nevertheless I went, in spite of threaten [sic] clouds, to

---

131   Edward Gibbon's *Decline and Fall of the Roman Empire.* In her memoir, Emma wrote that in summer 1863, she was knitting socks for soldiers while reading Gibbon, and had learned to do so effectively—an early example of what we today call "multi-tasking."
132   Edward Hitchcock's *The Religion of Geology and Its Connected Sciences* (1851). Hitchcock, a paleontologist, was a professor at Amherst College. Influenced by Georges Cuvier, he asserted that the earth was millions of years old some two decades before Darwin. Stephens makes no mention of the LeContes' knowledge of this important work. That Emma was reading it at her father's urging is of some significance (Stephens, *Science, Race, and Religion*).

see uncle John in the afternoon. He had a hard time with the Yankees—was not allowed a blanket to sleep on—no fire and had to march over a hundred miles with them. He saw one of his own negroes, Peter, on horseback, while he was plodding on foot. On the whole though he looks very well and feels more like himself except his foot.

Aunt Josie was sick in bed. Uncle John said that while he was marching along a Yankee officer rode beside him and asked: "What will you Southerners do when we have marched victoriously through Virginia and taken Richmond?" "I think Gen Lee may have something to say to that" he replied, "You have him to meet yet." "Well suppose we defeat & disperse his army?" "I suppose then we will have to resort to guerilla warfare."—The officer looked surprised and shocked—"Why can not you yield?" he asked—Uncle John shrugged his shoulders and said he would resort to anything rather than give up. "Well," said the Yankee, "I hope the South won't do anything of <u>that</u> kind, for of course in that event we would not spare or respect your <u>women</u>."

March 11th [Saturday]

A courier last night brought the news of the fall of Richmond—or at least of its evacuation—We have heard rumours to this effect for some time so we were in a measure prepared for it. It is so hard to believe—People talk about its being the best move—that now we will "catch" Sherman etc etc—It seems nonsense to me. The fact remains that our capital—the great bone of contention for which the Yankees have struggled in vain for four years—around which so many bloody battles have been fought—has fallen at last. I feel as if the end had come and utterly heartsick—and yet have become so accustomed to disaster, that nothing overwhelms me, not even this—It only somewhat deepens the gloom. We can not be conquered—that is unthinkable—but these are bitter days and we are passing through a dark cloud. Sherman marched through Georgia—Savannah fell—I thought he would be opposed here—The president promised to defend South Carolina—Sherman swept on unresisted, devastating, burning. He holds Charleston, has burned Columbia, left his whole track a smouldering desert—Now Richmond is fallen. Where is a way of hope? Only to Gen Lee and his poor little half starved army can the people look—Yet an army that has never suffered defeat, a contrast to the Western army.

Sunday March 12th

It is a calm bright spring day—warm, balmy and quiet. The campus is quite green with the springing grass and the tall elms are budding. The birds are singing again and as we walked home from church this morning we gathered blue hyacinths and yellow daffodils from among the blackened ruins.[133] Spring no longer looks gay and bright as it used to in this fair town buried in trees and gardens and even where the foliage is not destroyed the bursting green will make a sad contrast with the melancholy ruins. In church this morning all looked so familiar— the congregation full—Dr P. in his place again—choir and organ—that sitting there it was hard to realize all was so changed—coming out the ruins all around struck afresh with strangeness and unreality.

We have had some 120 of Wheeler's Cavalry here for a time but they are going to leave. They were drawn up in the street this morning with forage at their backs.

Yesterday morning I spent with aunt Jane who is in bed thickly broken out with measles, more consequences of Walter's visit to us with the measles—In the afternoon I went to see Miss Jane and Miss Sophia Reynolds and afterwards to Madame D'Ovilliers.[134] Nothing was talked of but that dreadful night. Poor little Madame! How she did jabber in her broken English—I will try to look up my friends but many left before the surrender and most of the rest are burnt out and I do not know where to find them. Some (among them the Carrolls & Bausketts)[135] went to Winnsboro and met the Yankees there.

March 14th [Monday]

Richmond has not fallen! Petersburg has been given up and Lee has drawn in his lines and sent 10000 men to Johnston. Aunt Jane

---

133   Emma reported accurately. Photographs of the ruins of Christ Episcopal Church show spring bulbs in bloom.

134   Emma's former teachers at the Columbia Female College. Emma described them in her memoir as "two maiden ladies—the elder a small, dried up, decidedly little lady—the younger her niece, gentler but very pious. Miss Jane taught English history, etc. Miss Sophia the sciences." Madame O'Ovilliers was the mother of Eugene D'Ovilliers.

135   See note 120 for the Carrolls. The Bauskett house was occupied by Col. Nathaniel Haughton. John Bauskett, formerly of Newberry and Edgefield, was a prominent lawyer (Scott, 34). He married Helen Niernsee, daughter of the architect John Niernsee. John's Bauskett's sister was Kate Bauskett, whom Emma called "an intimate friend" in her memoir (39). Emma noted that John Bauskett and Dr. Leland had houses in the same block that were not burned (73).

has heard from Cousin John. She has been uneasy about him for when he came that fatal Friday to tell her goodbye the Yankees were only two blocks behind him, at the State House. He barely escaped by the fleetness of his horse but had to ride 25 miles through a deserted country to join his command and thinks he would have starved but for the large lunch aunt Josie stuffed in his haversack as he left. Aunt Josie tried to look up some of our lost clothing. The authorities have taken everything stolen by the negroes or given them by the Yankees and exposed them in some building for identification by owners—Hearing that many articles were taken from Nitre Bureau negroes aunt Josie went forth with high hopes but all she recovered was a portion of one of her dresses and the flounce of my green embossed silk. She and cousin Lula lost even more heavily than mother and I in clothing for we only sent off our best things, but they sent everything except two winter dresses apiece and hardly a change of underclothing, and not an article to begin summer with. Our underclothing was all of homespun and our stockings home knit, so we kept them. The silk dresses so carefully treasured during the war are entirely irreplaceable. Aunt Josie & Cousin Lula lost 24 between them. How are we to get clothes when even calico is from $25 to $30 a yard? There is a report in town that Sherman has been killed but this is far too good to be true. Another report is that Hampton fell in with part of his wagon train and captured the citizens who left Columbia and recovered much silver stolen here. The Yankees said they had not anywhere met with such quantities of plate and valuables and plunder as they found in Columbia—that it seemed the richest place they had struck.[136] They told the people of Cheraw (which was also burned) that they had treated Columbia worse than they should have done, but Sherman told them when they crossed the river that he would not restrain them, but gave them license to sack, pillage and burn the "Capital of Secessia" as they chose.[137]

* * *

---

136   Citizens of the Lowcountry had also sent their valuables to Columbia for safe keeping.
137   Emma inserted a note here: "Several pages are missing here."

Saturday March 18th

We are looking for father home now. We expected him yesterday or today.

<u>At last</u> we have received some tidings from Charleston. Some people unable any longer to endure the state of things there have found their way on foot to Columbia. The reign of terror they describe is unparalleled even in this barbarous war. The city is garrisoned by negro troops who, unrestrained, perpetuate every barbarity—until at length their outrages reached such a pitch that officers were obliged to some extent to interfere—30 were shot for violating women. In the surrounding country—affairs are even worse than in the city—the slaves turned loose and wildest anarchy reigns. When some of Foster's[138] negro troops arrived in Georgetown the same excesses were begun there.[139]

A Mr. Middleton—80 years old, was ordered by ruffians to leave his house—He was alone, the family being here—He deprecated their cruelty urging that he was old and had never taken any part in the war. They said they knew he was a damned old rebel and ordered him to get out—He begged for a little time to move some effects—This being refused he went to his room, put a few clothes in a pillow case and taking a blanket from his bed left the house. The negroes took his blanket from him. He watched his burning house till it was consumed and then taking the road to Columbia, walked the entire distance from Georgetown, reaching this place a day or two ago.[140] The people are fearing that a

---

138   Miers identified Foster as Gen. John A. Foster, but it was actually John Gray Foster. General John G. Foster was given command of the U.S. Department of the South in May 1864, but was succeeded in command by General Quincy A. Gillmore in February 1865.

139   In March 1865 several companies of U.S. Colored Troops arrived as occupation forces in Georgetown, S.C. They subsequently began looting raids in the countryside. Adele Petigru Allston complained to a U.S. officer that her plantation Chicora Wood had been robbed of its furniture and provisions by freedmen and U.S. troops. (Easterby, *The South Carolina Rice Plantation,* 209). The first troops entering Charleston "were negroes under Colonel Bennett." On 21 February 1865, the 55th Colored Massachusetts landed and marched through the streets (*Harpers,* 18 March 1865).

140   Mr. Middleton was Henry Augustus Middleton, Sr., of Weehaw Plantation, outside Georgetown on Black River. He was born in 1793. Francis Kinloch owned Weehaw in 1760. His daughter Harriott married Henry Augustus Middleton, Sr. and had ten children. The sixth child, Henry, Jr., along with his brother Francis, was tending the great plantation garden before the war. He joined the Marion's Men of Winyah, a cavalry unit organized in 1861 by Governor Allston's eldest son, Ben (Elizabeth Allston Pringle's brother) , and was killed at First Manassas. As Emma reports, Middleton, Sr., was at Weehaw alone. The rest of the family was in Columbia. Henry's fourth daughter Harriott Middleton wrote a relative in March 1865: "Weehaw is gone—lying in ashes. Papa walked up here, though he got many a lift on the road. I mourn over Frank's [Francis Kinloch Middleton's] garden as I would over a dear friend,

negro garrison may be sent here. If such fears should be realized we must leave if we have to walk to Augusta. It is rumoured that the Yankee gunboats are coming up the river to complete their work of destruction of Columbia by blowing up the State House. We hear so many wild and dreadful rumours. Mrs Bird passed through yesterday on her way from Richmond to Augusta. She says the deepest despondency prevails there on account of the giving up of Charleston and Columbia and the expectation that Richmond will share the same fate. Charlotte still holds out—We know almost nothing—the only reliable news is from couriers and they come so rarely—It is wonderful the avidity with which every scrap of news or even rumour from the outer world is seized upon in this forlorn town.

Mr Pope[141] has just got in. He gives an amusing description of a week's experience in dodging Yankees. He says he only escaped by passing himself off as a preacher and was several times told by the Yankees that they had caught tax collector Pope. Most of them spoke exultingly of having burned Columbia—One only expressed regret because "it was such a pretty town." On his enquiring the cause of the conflagration, they at first repeated the story of the whiskey, but one fellow said frankly that he might as well tell the truth—that Sherman had ordered them to burn it, that they expected to burn it—that they <u>did</u> burn the hole of Secession—Mr Pope says they had not however expected to take it for Beauregard had telegraphed Hardee[142] to come to his aid and that scoundrel paid no attention to the telegram. Mr. Pope says all the Yankees he talked with concurred in unqualified admiration for the pluck and dignity of the Columbia women. Through all the frightful night they did not see a tear or hear one complaint and they did not think they could ever conquer the South if the men were animated by the same spirit as the women of South Carolina. Mr Pope asked them if they thought to whip the South by marching through,

---

and the Yankees cut down the oak trees everywhere. Susan—I know now what it is to hate! I believe that the destruction of Frank's garden has taught it to me" (Cheves-Middleton Papers, South Carolina Historical Society). A more detailed account is in Karen Stokes, *South Carolina Civilians*, 56-58). The detail of the soldiers cutting the avenues of live oaks and along the roads is corroborated in Elizabeth Allston Pringle's *Chronicles of Chicora Wood*. Pringle writes that the trees were heaped in piles and burned (See also, Patton Hash, *Carologue*, Spring 2000, 18.)
141   Joseph Daniel Pope, chief collector of Confederate taxes and head of the bureau for printing Confederate notes and bonds. Scott wrote, "Mr. Pope's record of an able, honest, and industrious and most efficient officer stands without a blot" (*Random Recollections*, 171).
142   General William J. Hardee.

devastating the country unopposed except by women & children. The Yankees replied that they did not expect to whip our armies but meant to starve us out. "And can you do that?" he asked. The Yankee said "Sometimes I doubt it, for everywhere we go we find such quantities of provisions. You Southerners have a rich country."[143]

Telegraphic communication will be opened with Richmond in a day or two and then I hope we will hear regularly from the armies in N. Carolina and Virginia and also what has become of Thomas. We are also soon to have a tri-weekly paper edited by Gilmore Sims and called "The Phoenix"![144] I had saved almost a regular file of daily papers from 1862 but in the confusion of the fire they were emptied out of the trunk scattered and destroyed. Mother tried to persuade me to go with her to the depot but had no wish [sic] to see the dreadful sight. The ruins are filled with the bones of the unfortunates and their mangled remains are scattered around.—The gas works too are destroyed beyond repair— When father comes back I think I will walk down to Granby and see the battlefield—though there is little to be seen I suppose beyond breastworks and earth torn up & trees cut by cannon balls. The last news from Johnston was that he had <u>retreated</u> to Raleigh. This arch-retreater will probably retreat till perhaps he retreats to Gen Lee who may put a stop to his retrograde movement.

* * *

April 1st

Since my last entry on the 18th ult. many events of importance have transpired—

About ten days ago father returned from Augusta bringing provisions, cloth, leather, and <u>tallow</u> to make some candles—thus far we had nothing but pine firelight after dark. The provisions were flour corn and bacon—a few hams but chiefly the sides—I am so sick of bacon—it

---

143   Southerners often cited Northern envy as a reason the war was waged.
144   William Gilmore Simms (1806-1870), the South's most important man of letters at the time, was an eyewitness to the burning of Columbia. His plantation in Barnwell had been burned shortly before Columbia. With Julian Selby, he edited *The Columbia Phoenix*, where he serialized his first version of *The Capture, Sack, and Destruction of the City of Columbia*. He reports how in rummaging through the ashes of the burned offices of the *South Carolinian*, he found a composing stick for typesetting, salvaged it, and used it to set type for the first issues of the new paper as a symbol of continuity. (See Kibler, "Simms's Editorship of the *Columbia Phoenix*.")

seems impossible for me to eat it. It seems as if I ought to when father and the rest can eat it and think it good, but indeed my stomach turns against it and I usually make my dinner of hominy, cornbread & butter. The cloth is six bolts of factory cloth, which father on account of his being a "Columbia sufferer" got at the very low price of only $3.00 a yard. It makes me groan in spirit to think of wearing this heavy stuff as underclothing all the hot summer. But as aunt Jane sagely observes, "It is better than wearing nothing." Indeed Cousin Ada and I agreed we would willingly wear sackcloth and even ashes if necessary rather than give up to the Yankees. With all ports closed we will be obliged to give up every foreign luxury, which are even now by their high prices beyond the reach of all but speculators. As I sat with Aunt Jane (sick with measles) we laughingly arranged it all and found we could live very well on home products—Our clothing is already mostly of homespun our stockings we already knit and we make our own gloves. Our hats we could plat from palmetto or grass and trim them in summer with natural flowers, in winter with holly berries and ivy. We have only a very few more things to learn in primitive dress. Father brought us some nice fine yarn so much pleasanter to us than the coarse stuff I got at the factory here and I am now knitting with it some beautiful stockings. It would seem very strange now to put on a pair of new store stockings. And I am such an accomplished knitter that I do not look at my work and so can read and study while I knit—My hands are rarely without my knitting except when otherwise employed and this has been a great resource during the long evenings with no light but the dim firelight— Father brought us also some coarse blankets—The tallow mother has moulded into candles. How we miss the gas! The evenings are so long and dismal by the light of a tallow candle. How unappreciated was this one luxury until we lost it! Mr Stovall spent several days looking about the miserable wreck of Columbia.

* * *

We hear all sorts of vague rumours about Johnston defeating Sherman but nothing definite enough to pin a hope to.

April 13th

Columbia was in quite a panic a few days ago. A Yankee raid was at Kingsville and we feared it would shortly be here but they turned off towards Camden.[145] I heard a gentleman say he thought Columbia would be garrisoned this summer as a headquarters for sending out raids into the upper part of the state. They say there has been a fearful battle in Virginia, the most fearful of the war, that Lee has lost 20000 men and fallen back while Grant has lost 50,000[146]—We can ill afford to lose that number of men. All looks so dark and gloomy—I do not despair as many do, but I feel very sad and bitter when I think of the condition of our dear country! The South <u>will</u> not give up—I can not think that—but I look forward to years of suffering and grief—years of desolation and bloodshed. They say Charleston has fallen—Montgomery too and Selma—More than all Richmond. All we have are those two armies but outnumbered—if they are overthrown then follows the wearying guerilla fighting and all the atrocities and evils that follow in its train.

I suppose the Yankees are holding a great jubilee in Charleston today. Not long ago they had a most absurd procession described in glowing colours and celebrating the Death of Slavery—Abolitionists delivered addresses on the superiority of the black race over the white—Adam and Eve were black—so were Cain & Abel—but when the former slew his brother his great fright turned him <u>white</u>! Also "as Christ died for the human race so John Brown died for the negroes," etc etc. Today they intended raising their wretched flag over noble old Sumter and there was to be a great to do and fuss over it. Poor old Sumter—dear old fort! What a degradation![147] This day four long years ago! The joy,

---

145   This refers to Potter's Raid, an expedition led by General E. E. Potter which moved west out of Georgetown on 5 April 1865 chiefly for the purpose of destroying railroads between Florence and Sumter. Potter's forces destroyed the railroad at Kingville as well as the depot other structures there. They arrived at Camden on 17 April 1865.

146   Possibly the Battle of Five Forks, 1 April 1865, or more likely the Battle of Sayler's Creek on 6 April 1865, the last major engagement in Virginia. The numbers Emma reports were exaggerated, but the Confederates suffered heavy losses in this battle (about one fifth of Lee's forces was captured or became casualties).

147   On 14 April 1865 Major Robert Anderson raised the U. S. flag over fort walls leveled by four years of constant Federal bombardment. Adam Dahlgren began the victory celebration by ordering 21-gun salutes from all the ships in the harbor. The speaker's stand was surmounted by giant flower-covered arches on top of which perched a large golden eagle. Rev. Henry Ward Beecher of New York, younger brother of Harriet Beecher Stowe, gave the long-winded keynote address in which he stated "The nation not the States is sovereign," because the war had settled that issue once and for all. He proclaimed that for the Southerner, "the only condition of submission is *to submit.*" He had been among the strongest supporters urging Lincoln to

the excitement—How well I remember it—For weeks we had been in a fever of excitement—On the day the news came of the Fall of Sumter we were all sitting in the library at uncle John's. The bell commenced to ring. At the first tap we knew the joyful tidings had come. Father & Uncle John made a dash for their hats—Jules & Johnny followed—We women ran trembling to the verandah—to the front gate eagerly asking the news of passers-by. The whole town was in a joyful tumult. What could now rouse us from our dull apathy unless it were the certain news of an honourable peace. What changes—what a lifetime we have lived in the four years past!

* * *

I am studying German now and am working away at the grammar and translating Wilhelm Tell[148]—I have long wanted to get a reading knowledge of this language and have eyed wistfully the sealed treasures of German literature in the library. So my pleasure can be conceived when Mrs Leland[149] offered to teach me in return for reading French with her—She and I have a conversation lesson of an hour and a half with Madame [D'Ovilliers] on Mondays and Thursdays at 10 o'clock— On Wednesdays I read French with Mrs Leland and on Tuesdays and Fridays we have a German class—Mrs L giving us generally two hours as she has much leisure—Indeed I would be sorry to leave Columbia and the libraries with these nice plans on hand.

---

wage war on the South and he and his congregation purchased guns for the cause which they called "Beecher's Bibles." The fanatical abolitionist editor William Lloyd Garrison participated. Lincoln did not attend but sent his personal secretary. Lincoln was assassinated only hours after the long ceremony terminated. An albumen print of the ceremony which Emma describes appears in Richard McCaslin, ed., *Portraits of Conflict: A Photographic History of the Civil War in South* Carolina (286). For a detailed account of the event, see Stokes, *South Carolina Civilians* (95-96).

148   Friedrich Schiller's play.

149   Emma wrote in her memoir that Mrs. Leland was "an English woman who as an English governess in Germany for some years, finally met old Dr. Leland [probably Rev. Aaron W. Leland] in Canada, and attracted by the title 'Professor,' an exalted one in Germany, married the old widower and came to Columbia first at the breaking out of the war, where he was a professor in the Presbyterian [Columbia Theological] Seminary and living in a large house on the block near the Bausketts—two houses that were not burned in the fire. During the last year of the war Dr. Leland had a stroke of paralysis which left him a helpless bedridden on her hands, with no means of support but the big house....We read German classics—prose and poetry" (73-74). Mrs. Leland took occupation General Ames as a boarder. In 1854, Professor Leland had taken part in the discussion of the unity or diversity of the races. He sided with Agassiz and Nott (diversity) against Bachman (unity). Stephens calls him a "long-time" professor at the seminary (Stephens, *Science, Race, and Religion*, 201).

April 14th [Thursday]

I am so thankful that winter is gone finally and entirely—Cold weather means real suffering in many ways to us and bright spring is doubly welcome. She did not come coquetting as last year but as it were rushed into our arms. In the space of two weeks the trees burst into leaf—so rapidly that one could almost see them unfolding. By the first of April they were in full foliage—Those parts of town like the campus, that were untouched by the fire are now lovely with the delicate green of Spring. Among the ruins one sees long avenues of burnt and blackened trees—Now and then in mocking contrast one will stretch its leafy branches over a crumbling wall—And sometimes half or part of a tree has struggled into leaf and the rest stands bare and gaunt. Christ Church[150] was one of the last buildings burned—it makes a beautiful ruin—especially now when through the tall gothic windows and above the pointed walls one sees the waving foliage of Blanding St. Here in the campus nothing mars the Springtime beauty—it is lovely. I am sit [*sic*] in the front door and the afternoon is deepening into twilight. The grass is fresh and green under the majestic elms whose wide spreading, sweeping branches so black and fine show out in relief against the tender green of the young leafage. The oaks too are all out and so thick is the mass of verdure that from my bedroom windows I can not see across to the library building with its white columns. Just before me on the green lawn beneath a large elm is pitched a tent or large fly under which are lying half a dozen soldiers. At a little distance two fires are burning and around them are grouped others busily engaged in preparing their evening meal. These men are just from Camden—"So then," as Goethe says, "the old story of the year is being repeated again—We are come again, thank God, to its most charming chapter—the violets and May flowers are its superscriptions and vignettes. It always makes a pleasant impression on us when we open at these pages the book of Life."[151]—We, father, Cousin Ada and I, walked into the woods yesterday afternoon— We found the ground fairly carpeted with violets, phlox and other spring

---

150   Christ Episcopal Church, "the largest and handsomest Episcopal church outside Charleston." It was designed and built in 1858-1859 by the local architect George E. Walker. See Kibler, "Columbia's First Architect."
151   Johann Wolfgang von Goethe.

flowers. We gathered large bunches of them and sat a long time on the moss by the Rocky branch just where the water makes a mimic cataract over large rocks.—I am always so happy when I get into the country.

Saturday 16th [April]

We went out this morning to have our feet measured for shoes. Oliver's Shop is a genuine phoenix risen from its ashes[152]—He has built a frame building of two rooms around his old chimney. Coming back we passed through the State house yard picking our way over piles of rubbish—On every side a wilderness of granite and marble. Piles on piles of white and Tennessee marble blocks cracked, broken and smoke begrimed—Many blocks are crumbling to pieces—even the granite slabs are cracked and scaling—from the heat of the burning workshops and sheds. Hundreds of sculptured capitals lie broken and defaced.[153] In the midst rises the half finished Capitol seeming to look mournfully down on the destruction that surrounds it. In a remote part of the ground, behind some granite blocks, lies scattered the chimes of St. Michael's—one quite destroyed, all cracked by the heat.[154] Those historic bells—10 in number, considered the finest chime in the country. They were presented from the Mother country while South Carolina was a colony. When Charleston was taken by the British the bells were sent to England. After the war some say they were returned, others that they were brought back—Anyway they came back to Charleston and for 80 years played from St. Michael's tower. Two years ago, when bells were given to be moulded into cannon, they were sent here either for that

---

152   J. & A. Oliver's on Main Street. Simms reports it burned (67). The shoe store's owner John Oliver died in 1899.
153   One of the columns and two of these capitals were salvaged and rest as ornaments in the garden behind the South Caroliniana Library.
154   Emma wrote in her memoir: "The principal targets [in bombarding Charleston] were the church steeples—much damage was done ... St. Michaels' steeple was so often struck that the famous chimes were removed and sent up to Columbia for safety. These highly prized bells were presented to St. Michael's by Queen Anne long before the revolution & so inscribed. They were noted for their sweetness & tone. They were placed in the new state house yard under special sheds—along with the finished and unfinished stone work—Corinthian pillars and carvings" (30). For Federal sighting of the steeples in bombardment, see the account of Augustine Smythe, stationed in the steeple itself, in Karen Stokes, ed., *Days of Destruction* (2007). For a contemporary description of the damage to St. Philip's and St. Michael's spires and a story of the bells, see C. C. Pinckney, *Report of the Committee on the Destruction of Churches* (9-10). Pinckney notes that St. Philip's suffered more from the bombardment than St. Michael's.

purpose or for safe keeping while the city was under fire. They were placed in a building on the State House grounds and here they lie now.[155]

News came today that Camden was <u>not</u> taken by the raiders. So there is some chance of getting our rice after all. (Rice belonging to the Nitre Bureau.)

Gen. Lovell has been appointed to the command of the Department of South Carolina.[156] I hope he will infuse some spirit into our people and defend us from the Yankees.[157]

* * *

Thurs. April 20th

[Written after hearing of Lee's surrender & fall of Richmond]

* * *

(Armistice or truce (?) between) Gens Johnston & Sherman not to be broken without 48 hours notice. Couriers have been despatched to stop Stoneman's raid at Camden.[158] What it is I do not know but it can not bode good to us. Thus the grand army of Virginia which has heretofore never known defeat but has stood like some great rock against which the huge waves of our enemies have dashed themselves in vain is now melted away. All that is left is Johnston's small army cooped up between Grant's hordes on the one hand and Sherman's on the other. Wiser heads than mine say it must surrender, and then the waves will roll over us. The South lies prostrate—their foot is on us— there is no help. During this short truce we breath [*sic*] but——O who could have believed, who has watched this four years' struggle that it could have ended like this! They say <u>right</u> always triumphs but what cause could have been more just than ours? Have we suffered all—have our brave men fought so desperately and died so nobly for <u>this</u>? For

---

155   A note by Emma appears at the bottom of the page: "After the war these bells were sent to England & recast in the same foundry where they were originally cast and now hang in St. Michael's steeple."

156   Mansfield Lovell, mentioned in Mary Chesnut's diary as a Yankee sympathizer (*Diary from Dixie*, 217).

157   At this point Emma inserted the following note concerning her original 1865 diary: "Several pages are here missing. I do not know how many entries are lost but infer the date of the next which I copy as it begins."

158   Forces under the command of General George Stoneman did not raid into South Carolina until May 1865. General Potter's forces left Camden on 18 April 1865.

four years there has been throughout this broad land little else than the anguish of anxiety—the misery of sorrow over dear ones sacrificed—for nothing! Is all this blood spilled in vain? Will it not cry from the ground on the day we yield to these Yankees.[159] We give up to the Yankees! How can it be—How can they talk about it—Why does not the president call out the women if there are not enough men—We would go and fight too—We would better all die together.—Let us suffer still more, give up yet more—anything anything that will help the cause—Anything that will give us freedom and not force us to live with such people, to be ruled by such horrible and contemptible creatures—to submit to them when we hate them so bitterly. It is cruel—it is unjust—I used to dream about peace—to pray for it—but this is worse than war.—What is such peace to us! What horrible fate has been pursuing us the last six months? Not much farther back than that we had every reason to hope for success—What is the cause of this sudden, crushing collapse? I can not understand it. I never loved my country as I do now—I feel I could sacrifice everything to it—And when I think of the future—Oh God! It is too horrible.

What I most fear is a conciliatory policy from the North—that they will offer to let us come back as before—Oh, no—no!—I would rather we were held as a conquered province, rather sullenly submit and bide our time. Let them oppress, tyrannize, but let us take no favours of them—Let them send us away out of the country—anywhere away from them and their hateful presence. We are all very wretched. Poor father! He had Carrie in his arms just now but her innocent joy and laughter so grated upon him he had to send her away. It seems dreadful to see anyone smile. It seems impossible to utterly despair—if we did we would be even more miserable than we are—We feel instinctively that something must hap [*sic*] to avert our doom—It is so terrible as to be unthinkable—We have been so confident of final success that we can not believe we are conquered. What fresh misfortune will I have to chronicle tomorrow? I am too sick at heart to write any more.

---

159   In Genesis it is recorded that Abel's blood cried out to God from the ground after he was murdered by his brother Cain.

Friday [April 21st]

Hurrah! Old Abe Lincoln has been assassinated! It may be abstractly wrong to be so jubilant but I just can't help it[160]—After all the heaviness and gloom of yesterday this blow to our enemies comes like a gleam of light—We have suffered till we feel savage—There seems no reason to exult for this will make no change in our position, will only infuriate them against us. Never mind our hated enemy has met the just reward of his life. The whole story may be a Yankee lie—The despatch purports to be from Stanton to Sherman. It says Lincoln was murdered in his private box at the theatre on the night of the 14th (Good Friday—at the <u>theatre</u>). The assassin brandished a dagger and shouting "Sic semper tyrannis"—Virginia is avenged! Shot the president through the head. He fell senseless and expired the next day a little after 10[161]—The assassin made his escape in the crowd. No doubt it was regularly planned and he was surrounded by Southern sympathizers. "Sic semper tyrannis." Could there have been a better death for such a man! At the same hour nearly Seward's house was entered. He was badly wounded as also his son. Why could not the assassin have done his work more thoroughly. That <u>vile</u> Seward—he it is to whom we owe this war—it is a shame he should escape.[162]

I was at Mrs. Leland's saying my German when Mrs Snowden brought in the news.[163] We were all so excited and talked so much that Wilhelm Tell was quite forgotten. Our spirits had been so low that the least good news elevated them wonderfully, and this was so utterly unlooked for—took us so completely by surprise. I actually <u>flew</u> home

---

160   There was rejoicing at the assassination of Lincoln in the North as well as the South. Thomas DiLorenzo notes that Lincoln was "the most hated of all American presidents" because of his frequent violations of civil liberties in the North, and that he was routinely denounced there as a dictator and a bloody tyrant. (*The Problem with Lincoln,* 130).
161   President Lincoln was shot on the 14th but actually died the next morning at 7:22 a.m., not 10 o'clock. As he jumped from the theatre stage, John Wilkes Booth cried Virginia's motto, *Sic semper tyrannis* ("Thus always the fate of tyrants," the declaration of Brutus as he assassinated Caesar).
162   William Seward, U.S. Secretary of State. He was at home when Lewis Payne forced his way past Seward's son and stabbed him three times but did not kill him. Payne was executed for the attempt. Emma was as usual accurate in gauging the political scene. Seward was indeed a major accomplice in waging President Lincoln's war on the South.
163   Probably Mary Amarintha Yates Snowden (1819-1898), widow of Dr. William Snowden and founder of the Calhoun Monument Association in Charleston. Nell Graydon writes that Mrs. Mary Amarintha Yates Snowden carried 40 to 50,000 dollars in securities around with her during the burning, sewed into her skirts. (Graydon, 137). There is also a G. T. Snowden mentioned in Scott, p. 147.

and for the first time in, oh! so long I was trembling and my heart beating with excitement. I stopped in at aunt Josie's to talk it over. They were all in Aunt Jane's room. As soon as I reached the head of the stairs they all cried out. "What do you think of the news!" "Isn't it splendid" etc etc. We were all in tremor of excitement. At home it was the same. If it is only true. The first feeling I had when the news was announced was simply gratified revenge—the man we hated had met his proper fate—I thought with exultation of the howl it had by that time sent through the North and how it would cast a damper on their rejoicings over the fall of our noble Lee—the next thought was how it would infuriate them against us—and that was pleasant too. After talking it over the hope presented itself that it might produce a confusion that would be favourable—But there is scarcely any likelihood of that—he is scarcely important enough for that. Andy Johnson will succeed him—The rail-splitter will be succeeded by the drunken ass[164]—Such are the successors of Washington and Jefferson—Such are to rule the <u>South</u>!

Sic semper tyrannis! It has been in my head all day.

"Tremblez tyrans! et vous perfidies

L'opprobres de toutes les parties—

Tremblez! vos projets paracides

Vout <u>enfin</u> recevoir leur prix!"[165]

What exciting, what eventful times we live in!

Sunday April 23rd

Dr P. this morning preached a fine and encouraging sermon. He says we must not despair yet. But even if we should be overpowered—not <u>conquered</u>—the next generation would see the South <u>free</u> and independent.

There is another rumour in town to the effect that the French fleet has defeated the Yankee fleet and taken New Orleans. It is only a rumour and alas! I dare not believe it—The air is so full of rumours that

---

164   President Andrew Johnson, a former tailor, did succeed Lincoln, "the rail-splitter."
165   Lyrics from *La Marseillaise*, composed by Claude Joseph de Lisle in 1792. English: "Tremble, tyrants and you traitors / The shame of all parties, / Tremble! Your parricidal schemes / Will finally receive their prize!"

one does not know what to believe—they only keep us in a feverish state of uncertainty.

The more I think of Lee's surrender the harder it is to bear—<u>That</u> army—that General. We idolized Stonewall Jackson—we worshipped Lee. It is perhaps well that President Davis has so many enemies for if all loved him as the others something would happen to him too. How well I remember the death of Stonewall Jackson!—I can never forget my feelings when I heard it. We had heard he was very low, but I did not dream <u>he</u> <u>could</u> die. I was lying on the lounge alone in the library, when father came in looking very sad. "Emma" he said gravely, "Stonewall Jackson is dead." How I loved him—he was my <u>hero</u>. I then admired Lee as grand, magnificent, but Jackson came nearer my heart—There was mourning deep and true throughout the land when that news came.[166] Since then Lee has had the hero-worship—<u>all</u>—both his and Jackson's— though the dead hero will always be shrined in every Southern heart. But I am allowing old reminiscences to fill my mind and page—not so old either—only two years, but events have crowded so thickly that it seems a long long time ago. Our beloved Lee! Now the first crushing grief for the country is passed in some measure away, how deeply I feel for <u>him</u>—How he must suffer—not only the humiliation, but to hold his hands in this hour of his country's greatest need—What must it have meant to him to yield that sword! And what are we to do without him!

I can not feel hopeless. Today I do not feel as disheartened as I did last Thursday when the news came—the terrible news. We still have an army in the west—and dark as everything is we <u>must</u> hope. The conviction that the South <u>can not</u> be conquered, that it can <u>never</u> be re-united with the North, is so deeply rooted in my heart—Since the war began that conviction has never been shaken once till last Thursday— then I was so overwhelmed by the thought of Lee's surrender that there seemed no ground under my feet—even now there can be no hope but in foreign aid—But something <u>must</u> turn up—help <u>must</u> come. "The darkest hour's before the dawn."—If there should be no dawn!————

* * *

---

166   Emma wrote in her memoir: "I will never forget the grief of that 10th of May [1863] with its tragic news….I shut myself in the parlour and wept as if my heart would break" (31).

May 2nd

My last entry was not quite ten days ago—it seems like months—we have suffered so much since—Then we were buoyed up by the hope of foreign intervention and Lincoln's assassination. It was confidently affirmed that our President had said in a speech at Charlotte that the French had promised intervention and our darkest days were passed. I do not know that the president ever made a speech there, or said such words, but we believed it—A thousand rumours filled the air now that the French fleet was at New Orleans—now at Beaufort now at Georgetown, and finally it was confidently stated that this ubiquitous fleet had defeated the Yankees in Hampton Roads. I will <u>never</u> believe another French rumour nor any other rumour that means hope to this unhappy land—Nothing good can come—fate has heaped upon us miseries & misfortunes that could not even have been dreamed of by us—the only question now is not "What hope?" but "What new bitterness?"

On the Sunday night of my last entry, I think it was the 23rd Cousin Willie[167] came from Europe by way of the North—succeeding at last in reaching his native land—eager to join her struggle for freedom. In what condition does he find her?—Monday morning I was returning from my French when Sallie called me in to the library to see him. I found a boy of 19—rather short with a pleasant and real "Le Conte" face. I was prepared to like him because of the patriotism that sent him to a failing cause.—We did not rush very fast into an acquaintanceship, both being rather shy—but I like him better every day and if he stays here long enough I think we will be good friends. He spent a week at Aunt Josie's and then came over here where he still is.

Wednesday May 17th

I have not touched my journal for two weeks—When I tried to chronicle the painful events transpiring, I found I could not. It would

---

167   William LeConte (1846-1876), the son of Joseph's brother Louis Eaton LeConte, Sr. (1821-1851) and Harriet Nisbet Le Conte (1824-1892). Emma wrote in her memoir, "Aunt Harriet spent some years in Europe—went over before the war to educate her children (William, Eva Harriet (1844-1911), Louis Jr. (1849-1883), and John Nisbet (1848-1925)] and remained until the last year of the same when exchange became difficult and she was forced to return to Washington. I mentioned in my diary how Willie walked his way South to join the Confederate Army (79). Harriet and her children lived in Washington, D.C. (1851-1858), Europe (1858-1864), and came back to Washington in 1865, as Emma writes.

not only take so much time but perhaps it is best not to put all I felt and suffered on paper—One of these days I may think those feelings were wicked. The fall of the Confederacy so crushed us that it seemed to me I did not care what became of me—It is impossible not to feel rebellious and bitter—it is impossible not to feel that it is unjust and cruel—And so I had better not write about it all—only of personal and family matters—if I can keep back the expression of what fills my heart and thoughts.

* * *

The troops are coming home. One meets long absent familiar faces on the streets, and congregations once almost strictly feminine are now mingled with returning soldiers—Our boys, Cousin Johnny and Julian—have come home too. It was pleasant to see them again but the meeting was more sad than glad. We would have waited many years if only we could have received them back triumphant. For four years we have looked forward to this day—the day when the troops would march home. We expected to meet them exulting and victorious—That was to be a day of wildest joy, when the tidings of peace should reach us. And the thought of that time used to lighten our hearts and nerve us to bear every trial and privation. Then we determined, after our independence was acknowledged and the time came for Gen Lee to disband his army, to go on to Richmond to see the glorious sight—to see the hero take leave of his brave victorious men. The army is disbanded now—oh! Merciful God!——the hot tears rush into my eyes and I can not write.

* * *

Cousin Johnny came first, and about a week later, Julian. We were not expecting Jule so soon. It was a lovely moonlight night and we— both households—had agreed to walk together over the town and view the ruins by the full moon—We had not gone more than two or three blocks when we met a rough soldier with knapsack and blanket roll on his back. The meeting may be better imagined than described. After much embracing, kissing, chattering and some tears, Julian, who was too tired to go with us went on home to his mother accompanied by uncle John and Johnny, while the rest of us pursued our walk—Cousin John came home quite broken down but Jule seems very well except that his feet are so blistered he can hardly walk. He is of course paroled.

I must say something of that walk among the ruins—It was very beautiful and melancholy. I wish I had a picture of that scene— Everything was still as death—the only sounds that broke the silence were our footsteps among the rubbish and sometimes the low voices of our party—there was little talking—the weird scene seemed to cast a spell upon us. As far as the eye could reach, only spectre like chimneys and the shattered walls, all flooded over by the rich moonlight which gave them a mysterious but mellow softness and quite took from them the ghastly air which they wear in the sunlight—There only lacked moss and lichen and tangled vines to make us believe we stood in some ruined city of antiquity—We walked down Sumter Street and turned into Blanding— This was still more beautiful for the handsome residences made most picturesque ruins—Clarkson's house with its columns gleaming in the moonlight looked like an old Greek ruin[168]—And for some reason, perhaps the large lots & greater distances between the houses, the trees and shrubbery on this street have been almost unscorched, and make masses of foliage about the crumbling walls. At last we reached Christ Church—It was a very pretty little church and makes a lovely ruin— it was charming in this mystic light. As we stood before it, the moon shone full upon us through the big arched window—We stood gazing on it in silence for many minutes. Had the walls only been mantled with ivy and a few sharp outlines softened by time & clinging lichens it would have been perfect. The walls are entire almost and firm—and we went up the stone steps and viewed the interior from the entrance. Retracing our steps, we walked across to Main St. and walked down that former thoroughfare, trying to imagine it as it once was—We took a peep up the tall tower of the market and sat on the fallen bell. As we walked down the middle of the street the great State house shone white before us looking itself like a grand ruin. We would have liked to have taken a comprehensive view from the top of its walls but the Yankees had burned out the temporary floors and stair steps, leaving only the walls like a shell. We had started out at eight and it was ten when we got to Aunt Josie's and found Julian waiting for us quite tired and anxious to get to bed.

We enjoy having the boys back and in spite of all depressing influences have pleasant days. Young people can not be depressed and

---

168   See note 96.

gloomy <u>all</u> the time. There are eight of us altogether between the ages of 14 and 24 and it is nice to have the boys home even if they are returned like this—We walk in the woods afternoons—generally down to Gregg's Spring[169] where we sit and laugh and talk and teaze [*sic*] each other till almost dark. The last two afternoons we walked to the river. Cousin John Harden[170] and Willie leave us next Monday—the former goes to the plantation, the latter to his uncle Gen. M. L. Smith in Athens[171]— And we resolve that this last week of their stay shall be a merry one— they promised to meet here every evening for a dance. Accordingly Monday evening the whole contingent from the other house came over and we had a jolly time. Tuesday evening was if anything even livelier. Our spirits seemed to rise at the sound of the piano and we went into it with a vim—especially cousin John—How long it had been since any of us had danced! It did seem heartless perhaps but we could not help enjoying it—and it seemed such a relief to throw off the trouble and gloom for a little while—and it was only among ourselves. I will be sorry when two of the cousins leave us—We will miss them so much and it will be very dull without them. Jule is quieter and Johnny is much younger[172]—and the girls will predominate—now we are evenly divided.

Thursday [May 18th]

We were visited yesterday by a squad of Yankees under a Lieutenant Brett—the first that have been in Columbia since the 20th of February. They bring a message to Magrath—Magrath with the fate of the Gov. of North Carolina before his eyes had "skedaddled." Thereupon the blue devils fastened their horses and set themselves down in the campus to await his return. The negroes throng around them and they afiliate [*sic*] pleasantly with their coloured brethren—even affectionately—They lie beside them on the grass and walk the streets with the negro girls calling them "young ladies." And why not? Doubtless they recognise in them not only their equals but their superiors—<u>perhaps</u> negroes <u>may</u> come in contact with them without being degraded and contaminated, but I doubt it, for the negro is an imitative race. He has been elevated

---

169   Now Columbia's Maxcy Gregg Park, named in honour of Columbia native, General Gregg.
170   Aunt Josie's son (1839-1902) of the LeConte plantation in Liberty County, Georgia. Joseph rented his Georgia plantation to nephew John Harden in 1866.
171   General Martin Luther Smith (1819-1866) of Athens, Georgia.
172   Julian was 20 and Johnny 15.

to some extent but will no doubt quickly retrograde in association with such white people as these.

Dear me! How the sight of that blue uniform makes my blood boil! They are camped just in front of the house so that I can not go to the front windows without seeing their hateful forms, and the sight fills me with such horrid feelings that I keep in the back parlour & dining room and close my blinds when I go to my bedroom. Yesterday I went into the library for a book. The sash-door was open and I saw them sitting and lying about on the grass.—Before I knew it my hands were clinched [*sic*] and I ground my teeth and such a feeling came into my heart as startled me and I fled upstairs away from the sight of them. These men seem to be the meanest type of the mean nation. Their presence has put an end to our pleasant evening re-unions—to our walks, in fact to everything.

Afternoon

This morning we received the last crowning piece of bad news—I did not think it possible anything worse could happen—We heard of the capture of President Davis![173] This is dreadful not only because we love him but because it gives the final blow to our cause. If he could have reached the west he might have rallied the army out there and continued the resistance—but now, where can we look for a head? I was studying my German when father came in and told me—I laid my head on the table without a word—I did not cry—the days of weeping are past—but oh! the heartache—The only thing left to hear now is the surrender of the army in the west and that must come pretty soon—I think I have given up hope at last—at least for the present—We will be conquered—only in the future can we still hope—either for a foreign war in which we can join the enemies of the United States, or else that after years of recuperation we may be strong enough and wiser by experience, renew the struggle and throw off the hateful yoke. The only other chance is that by their oppression and insolence they may drive the people to guerilla warfare and be wearied out at last.

---

173   Confederate President Jefferson Davis was captured at Irwinville, Georgia on 10 May and placed in chains and under constant guard at Fortress Monroe. He was not allowed a chair or privacy at any time. The Irish nationalist John Mitchel, a fellow prisoner at Fortress Monroe, called Davis's cruel, humiliating imprisonment "one of the blackest villainies known to history." (*New York Daily News,* 13 June 1865)

Tuesday May 24th

Gov. Magrath arrived Saturday and on Sunday morning the Yankees left town carrying some 300 negroes with them. The message to Magrath was in regard to his proclamation about seizing Confederate property. It seems the Yankees took this in high dungeon, regarding it as theirs—

We took our last walk together on Monday afternoon and our last little dance Monday evening, for they did not leave till this morning, but I do think our hearts were much in it for we could not but feel sad at the approaching parting. They started at 5 a.m. to walk to Augusta and I was up to see them off. I miss Cousin Willie very much. He has been in the house so long that he seemed quite one of us and I have grown very much attached to him.

An order was sent to Gen Lovell for distribution. The sense was as follows:

["]Whereas one Magrath[174] styling himself Governor of South Carolina has issued a proclamation ordering the seizure of all Confederate property within the limits of the State: —

And whereas one Joseph Brown styling himself Governor of Georgia has published an order convening the legislature. And whereas one [A. K.] Alison styling himself Governor of Florida has taken steps for the election of a governor for that State:—

Be it known to all citizens of the aforesaid States that such orders and proclamations are null and void, and that the status of said States will hereafter be decided by the proper authorities and and at the proper time."—

And "that the slaves are to be considered free but are advised to work as before for their former masters as the United States will not tolerate idleness." It is signed Gilmore—[175]

Is this not insolent? Gen. Lovel [*sic*] put it in his pocket and refused to give it circulation.[176]

---

174   South Carolina Governor Andrew G. Magrath was arrested by Federal authorities on May 25, 1865, and imprisoned at Fort Pulaski, Ga.

175   General Quincy A. Gillmore, commander of the Union's Department of the South.

176   A notice in the 2 May 1865 issue of the *Columbia Phoenix* is a special order assigning Brig. Gen. Albert Blanchard as the commandant of the "Fort at Columbia" and relieving Col. A. F. Butler, by command of Maj. Gen. Lovell, and signed by John M. B. Lovell, A.A.A.G."

Sunday May 28th

I do not attempt to write regularly now—I have lost all interest in keeping this fragmentary record—in fact in <u>everything</u>—I must try to get interested again in studying and reading—try to get my thoughts away from the country. It is very hard to do this—such things have so long been neglected—I have lost interest and I think father has too— During this long vacation he has asked me once or twice why I do not commence again, but I can see he is indifferent—We are all indifferent and nothing short of excitement can rouse interest in anything. Yet I feel I must study—An education now is more important to me than ever—The only work I can look forward to is teaching and I ought to be studying all I can. I have not been absolutely idle for I have continued to teach Sallie regularly.

Last Thursday the garrison arrived.—It consists of one regiment under Col. Horton[177] another is expected shortly. Col Horton and his men are Westerners—He seems to be a gentleman and his men are under strict discipline. They molest no one and are polite. I am glad to say they are introducing some order in town—it is sadly needed—and setting the negroes to work. These men, so far from fraternizing with the negroes, seem to hold them in profound disgust.[178] The people avoid them and have nothing to do with them except on business, neither do they offer them any form of insult. The regiment is encamped back of the campus, but one company comes inside every morning as a guard to Col H. who has his headquarters in the campus a few doors from our

---

The 1 May 1865 issue of the *Columbia Phoenix* announced that "Maj. Gen. Mansfield Lovell is assigned to command in the State of South Carolina." Emma likely refers here to Mansfield Lovell. Earlier in her diary, on 16 April, Emma noted that "Gen. Lovel" had been appointed to the command of the Department of South Carolina. See note 151.

177   This is Col. Nathaniel Haughton, 1833-1899, of the 25th Ohio Infantry, the commandant of the occupation garrison in Columbia. Emma spells his name Horton on several occasions but later refers to him as Col. Haughton. His arrival and early activities are noted in the *Columbia Daily Phoenix,* 12 July 1865.

178   Other sources agree that the soldiers from the Midwest scorned African-Americans, felt them to be the cause of the war, and resented their competition economically. Simms wrote: "The Western men, including the Indiana, and a portion of the Illinois and Iowa, were neither so dexterous nor unscrupulous—were frequently faithful and respectful; and, perhaps, it would be safe to assert that many of the houses which escaped the sack and fire, owed their safety to the presence of the contiguity of some of these men. Ruder of speech and manner than the Eastern men, rough and surly perhaps, they lacked equally the impudence, pretension, pomposity, and utter indifference to truth, honesty, and shame, which distinguished the latter" (*Sack and Destruction,* 63). Alfred Huger also testified to the kindness of two "Western men" who helped save his burning house amid wholesale pillage and arson. They (Goodman and Elliott) were from Indiana and Iowa (Huger, "The Burning of Columbia").

house.—So we still have them before our eyes. The soldiers behave so well—indeed there are guards on every street—that ladies are beginning to walk freely out when it is absolutely necessary. I only go out to my lessons and occasionally to aunt Josie's—The first time I went out to my German, it was almost amusing. There has been a sentinel at the campus gate and as I had the same invincible horror of passing him that one would have to a very loathsome reptile, I thought I would go through aunt Josie's yard into the street, but when I got beyond the gate I saw there were two standing between me and her side gate. I hesitated, walked very slowly, hoping they would move off. I started to turn back but mother was in the door watching and laughing at me. So I doubled my veil, raised my parasol and passed swiftly and boldly between them for they were several yards apart. I have grown a little more used to them after several days but I still feel a shudder when I pass within 20 yards of one. Consequently I always avoid the guard at the gate by going across through Aunt Josie's. This morning though I went through with the rest of the family going to church and was obliged to pass so near one who was sitting on the ground that I had to hold my skirts back for fear my dress might accidentally brush him.

Listen! They are beating tattoo now—that disgusting Yankee doodle! And they have dress parade every afternoon just opposite the campus.[179]

Monday [May] 29th

I went to French this morning. These conversation lessons are very pleasant but I do not know how long I can be allowed to enjoy them. True Madame's prices are very low but when it is all we can do to live, anything is high. I pay her in provisions at the rate of 10 cts an hour, but our supply is diminishing very fast and we can not tell where more is to come from. Poor father is looking very badly too and is very much troubled—he can get no employment and not one cent of money in the house. He hopes when the railroad is completed there may be some trade and business here and he can then get work but that will be quite a while yet. In the meantime a flatboat belonging to the Nitre

---

179   This parade ground existed until the 1960s when it became a parking lot and reflecting pool for Edward Stone's Undergraduate Library, now the Thomas Cooper Library. It was then also used as a track for physical education classes in the early 1960s.

bureau has been secured to father by Uncle John in payment of salary due—this through the kindness of Horton, to whom father went to ask that it be not confiscated but that he allow it to be disposed of in this way.[180] James Gibbes[181] wants father to bring up corn for the city with this boat, and the tithe that he gets therefore will keep our two families for a while. It is pretty bad but I do not think we will starve. We have been very low down several times but something always turns up at the last moment.

They are administering the oath here now and almost everyone is obliged to take it for unless they do they are not allowed to engage in any occupation, nor to travel beyond the limits of the town, nor will they be protected against violence or injustice of any kind. Aunt Josie says, and I suppose they reason in the same way, that she would take it as a mere form forced upon her and therefore not binding on her conscience and that she would break it as readily as she would take it. But I can not feel that way and I do not see how I could do it unless really starving. Father too feels it would be a most painful necessity that would compel him to such a humiliation. Well I do not suppose it will be required of women and I hope father will be spared the swallowing this bitter pill on account of his being a paroled officer. I saw a copy of the oath yesterday. It requires you to repudiate all allegiance to the so-called Confederate States and only permits loyalty to your own State as long as that State is not opposed to the United States—thus putting allegiance to the U.S. government <u>above</u> that to the <u>State</u>. You then have to swear allegiance to the U.S. government binding yourself in the most solemn way to uphold it under all circumstances and all this is sworn "without mental reservation or secret evasion, so help me God." Who could take such an oath as that? It is a tyrannical measure to force it upon the Southern people. Ministers are not allowed to preach without taking it and I hear Mr Shand[182] has had to submit to it. If we could <u>only</u>

---

180   At the bottom of this page of the diary, Emma noted: "Father was consulting chemist of the N. B. [Nitre Bureau]. Uncle John was superintendent of the N. B. works at Columbia."

181   James Guignard Gibbes, son of Dr. Robert W. Gibbes.

182   Reverend Peter Shand, Jr., gave up the study of law to become the rector of Trinity Episcopal Church. He served from 1834 to 1886. Simms wrote, Reverend Shand "sought in vain to save a trunk containing the sacred vessels of his church. It was violently wrested from his keeping, and his struggle to save it only provoked the rougher usage" (62). When Reverend Shand refused to pray for the president of the United States, his church was closed and turned over to an African-American congregation.

leave the country—Will we ever have the means to do so? How could we ever raise the money? We dream of this and make plans to emigrate—but the means are lacking now. We will have to wait—but I would rather work hard for my daily bread than live in luxury under Yankee rule.

These Yankee officers who behave like gentlemen—if Yankees <u>can</u> be gentlemen—take it rather hard that they are treated so coldly and allowed no social intercourse with the citizens. Horton especially seems to feel it that he is cut off so absolutely from the society of ladies. Great heavens! What do they expect? They invade our country, murder our people, desolate our homes, conquer us, subject us to every indignity and humiliation, and then we must offer our hands with pleasant smiles and invite them to our houses, entertain them perhaps with "Southern hospitality."—All because sometimes they act with common decency and humanity! Are they crazy? What do they think we are made of?[183]

June 27th

A whole day before me to read without interruption—what a luxury! Mrs Leland told me when I called for her to go to Madame's yesterday that she would not be able to meet her German class this afternoon so I have not those 12 or 14 pages of German to translate and can put the time into reading besides having the whole afternoon to myself. I have made up my room and finished with Sallie's lessons and with my books before me can not linger long over this I think. In history I am still on old Gibbon but getting through him as fast as I can as I am anxious to begin Michelet's "Histoire de France."[184] I happened to be reading on Mahomet & his doctrines so have dipped into the Koran which I will read through—<u>if I can</u>. I am also reading a volume of Carlyle's Essays.[185]—I like Carlyle <u>very</u> much. I am getting back to my books all right as far as reading is concerned—I begin again to find them a blessed resource—to be able to lose myself in their world and forget the world of trouble around me—But when it comes to study—I do not find it so easy—In the long interval, I seem to have lost the power of close application and systematic regularity—and with no outside stimulus it is pretty hard—

---

183   At the end of her entry for 29 May, Emma inserted this note: "There is a hiatus here of about a month. I do not know where some pages are lost or whether there were no entries made."
184   Jules Michelet (1798-1874), *Histoire de France,* first published in 1855.
185   Thomas Carlyle (1795-1881), *Critical and Miscellaneous Essays,* a series of volumes, the first of which was published in 1838.

But I have made a start—Till father can again give me instruction, I have decided to review Arithmetic and Algebra with a view to possibly being able to get an assistant teacher's place. The higher mathematics I do not think it will be necessary to freshen up on as I would not be expected to teach them at my age. It may not be necessary for me to get work and I may not be able to get it but the review can do no harm in any event—I wish I could get some employment now—anything no matter what—if I only cold make a little money—ever so little, just to help father a little bit—We subsist now on the little father makes from his flatboat. He brings up corn for the town and gets a tenth which is divided between him and Uncle John and Capt Green—We hope for a little improvement in business when the railroad is finished.

Gen Hartwell [186] is in town again—the vile miserable tyrant—He came up here not long ago—I suppose he thought things were going on too smoothly and comfortably under Haughton and he was needed to stir up a fuss and make the people realize their position—He is a friend of Prof Pierce and immediately called on uncle John to deliver messages from him and make enquiries. The first thing he did was to take possession of Mrs. Bauskett's house which she had left for a short visit to her plantation. And there he established himself and proceeded to hold his orgies. The next thing he did was—to go to church. After the service he wrote a note to Mr. Shand saying he had observed the omission of the prayer for the President of the United States and that "Mr. Shand would be pleased to use it hereafter or he would be under the unpleasant necessity of closing his church." N.B. Closing a church at present means giving it to the negroes.

A few days after, he left for a week or two. Mr Shand went to Col Haughton about it—The colonel told him he was very sorry but since the thing was brought before him officially he was compelled to carry out his orders. "I have" he said "abstained from going to church ever since I have been here, because I understood the prayer was not used and I did not wish to interfere with your religious worship." The next Sunday Col Haughton went to church and the prayer was used. At the first words the congregation rose from their knees—Mr Shand hurried through it as if the words choked him and at end not one amen was

---

186   General Alfred S. Hartwell. His regiment was stationed between Orangeburg and Columbia, and he ran the district office of the Freedmen's Bureau.

heard throughout the church, not even from the minister who was assisting at the altar. Cousin Lula says she felt her blood begin to boil as she heard that villainous wretch prayed for! Did ever anyone hear of such tyranny as forcing a <u>prayer</u> on people—What has the government to do with the church? There is no union of church and state in this country!—

Gen Hartwell has called on Uncle John again this time. He mentioned that he wished to provision the town and relieve the suffering here—that he could bring supplies to Fort Mott[e] by steamer but would need boats to transport them to Columbia. Father accordingly went to see him to try to make arrangements for hiring his boat to him. He is very willing to take it. As father went out, in order to apologize, as it were, for his deep anxiety, he remarked that this seemed a piddling sort of business to be so much interested in and one in which he had never been accustomed to engage. "But" he added, "the fact is General the subsistence of our two families depends on it." The remark seemed to strike Hartwell and I suppose he thought on it. At all events he called on Uncle John in the afternoon and offered to lend either of them as much money as they wished. He said he knew it was a delicate offer to make and he was fully aware of the bitterness of feeling that existed at present but if they hesitated to accept it from him, at least they might draw on Pierce[187] and he would honour the draft. Of course his offer was declined—as long as we can keep body & soul together Father would not borrow from anybody but to be under obligations to a <u>Yankee</u>!——

We have corn, a little flour and a few vegetables from the garden. For several weeks we have not had any meat until the past three days. Mother has bought a little bacon with the proceeds of her buttermilk but I can not eat bacon especially this hot weather [*sic*]—Yesterday we had a little piece of beef—a luxury indeed—the first we have tasted since Sherman passed through. It is the last of June but we have had no fruit except blackberries and wild plums, although I hear it is a plentiful fruit season. Madame gave me three large figs yesterday. The Yankees are issuing rations but they are only drawn by people in actual need or who have no self respect.—

---

187   Probably Professor Benjamin Peirce , a friend of the LeContes at Harvard in 1850, and still close. Peirce was one of several scientists who recommended Joseph LeConte for a position at the University of California in 1869.

Jane left us yesterday having only informed mother the day before of her intended departure. She was a great nuisance, but her leaving so unexpectedly caused us some inconvenience as we have to take care of Carrie—If she can get a nurse for her food she will do so and we will do the housework between us. I wish she could clear out the whole of them—We have them to feed and get very little out of them in return.

Wednesday [June 28th]

We have had unprecedented rains, but yesterday the sun came out to the joy of everyone. I walked in the afternoon to the park with Lawrence Reynolds[188] and after tea Mr & Miss B. called—Mr B. is very pleasant but not I judge overladen with brains—Sallie and some of her friends had two dances here last week, on Wednesday and Friday evenings— Both evenings were rainy and I had to join in to help them out. Cousins Lula & Ada came over Friday evening to look on—Lawrence came and played for them on his violin which however was minus one string—a deficiency that could not be supplied—and some of the music was in consequence rather curious. Mr Hayne[189] dropped in later and we made a group of older folks in the back parlor while the juveniles danced in the front.

When Hartwell came back the other day he brought a Gen Hatch[190] with him—So they are both at Mrs. Bauskett's who as soon as she heard of the state of affairs hurried back to Columbia and calling on Gen Hatch demanded her house. He treated her insolently—She spoke her mind rather freely and he threatened to arrest her. He got spiteful and declares [sic] she shall not have her house at all. The two tyrants leave Columbia next week I think. It is almost impossible to tell of all they do, and besides we are grown so used to it now.—

---

188   The son of Reverend John Lawrence Reynolds (1814-1877), Professor of Roman Literature at South Carolina College, whose family shared the duplex. Emma wrote in her memoir that their quarters "were not a stone's throw apart," and she and Lawrence became great friends after the war. She said they "had grown up together." It was Lawrence who was one of her first escorts to dances (Memoir, 68-69).

189   Likely one of the sons of Charlestonian Issac William Hayne (1809-1880), South Carolina's attorney general from 1848-1868. The most probable candidate is Theodore Brevard Hayne (1841-1917). He married Lilah Adams, a LeConte in-law, and they lived in Columbia. His carte de visite from February 1867 in civilian clothing appears in *Mary Chesnut's Civil War Photograph Album*, 194-195. The date is mistranscribed in the album as 1861. Theodore Hayne was an officer in the Confederate Army.

190   General John P. Hatch.

July 5

Yesterday the negroes had their grand celebration which has been talked of for the past two months. The white people shut themselves within doors and the darkies had the day to themselves—they and the Yankees. It was a fearfully warm day and some 4000 or 5000 negroes assembled in Columbia. To prevent any disturbance Gen Haughton ordered two regiments who were on their way up the country to stop on the other side of the river until after the fourth. Most of the gentlemen of the town were invited but of course not one <u>real</u> gentleman was present. Father's invitation was given him last Thursday and when I came in from Madame's mother handed it to me saying "Let us see what she will say." She and father were greatly amused at the expression of surprise and then of supreme scorn that overspread my face as I read. I was highly indignant and regarded it as a piece of insolent <u>impudence</u> but father said he thought it was meant kindly.

I had dreaded the cannonading, for it was said 80 blank cartridges were sent up for the occasion and the cannon was to be planted in the campus gate. I expected to be aroused by daylight but was agreeably disappointed for not one was fired the whole day—I could have listened to the roar of cannon at our very door all day long and thought it music were it celebrating <u>our</u> independence and——but well, well—what is the use of talking about it—

The immense procession was marshalled down until it reached the College Hall[191] where they listened to addresses from Col Haughton, an abolition lawyer from Philadelphia, and two or three negroes. The poor old Hall where the students used to spout at their commencement, and where at the beginning of the war when they organized as the "College Cadets" was presented to them with much speechifying the flag given by the ladies. O who could have imagined its being put to <u>this</u> use!— Such horrid degradation!

On this occasion it was decorated with flowers by negro girls and <u>that</u> gay and refined audience was replaced by a motley throng of negroes and the poor old stage where Capt Gary[192]—young and

---

191   An impressive Neo-Roman temple at the south terminus of Sumter Street, less than a block from the LeConte house, built in the late 1850s as the college chapel and a place for other large audiences. It is now called Longstreet Theatre.
192   John H. Gary, captain of the South Carolina College Cadet Company in 1861. He led his

enthusiastic—poor fellow, he long ago filled a bloody grave—banner in hand spouted fire and fury about patriotism and swore so many things about their flag—Think in contrast of these orators!

After all the speeches were ended—I hear Col. H gave them some very wholesome[193] advice—they repaired to their dinner which was spread in the woods just out of town. The dinner was on a grand scale and after it was over the guests began dancing. They had asked Col Haughton's permission to follow the example of the Charleston negroes and bury Slavery with pomp and ceremony but the colonel refused advising them to wait till they were absolutely certain they were free permanently before burying Slavery. Thanks to Col. H everything was quiet and orderly and but for the crowds and dust one would not have imagined the fourth was being celebrated. After nightfall they returned and from the common opposite the campus[194] sent off fireworks while a brass band played continuously. I watched the fireworks from the front door for a little while but I could not stand it—it was too humiliating and made me realize our condition too keenly. When the pyrotechnics were exhausted the band ceased and the negroes were left to make their own music. Hundreds of voices singing strange negro songs and hundreds of feet dancing weird negro dances made a terrible noise. They were still dancing when Col Haughton returned about twelve o'clock and putting an end to their frolic we were able to sleep.

We are very fortunate in having Col Haughton. As far as lay in his power he has tried to reduce the anarchy and confusion to something like order. He has been all kindness and consideration to the citizens. The negroes dislike him and say he is no Yankee but half a rebel. It goes against the grain to admit anything good of a Yankee, but I have to own that he has acted well towards us. He is a Western man which may partly account for it. Like all Westerners he is rough unpolished and not highly educated but he seems to have the instincts of a gentleman, and although he evidently feels the coldness with which he is treated

---

unit to Charleston, where they served during the bombardment of Fort Sumter. Under fierce attack in Battery Wagner, Gary was mortally wounded when he picked up a lighted shell lobbed into the fort, and threw it out. It exploded while it was still too close. He died 5 days later on 17 August 1863. A carte de visite image of Gary appears in *Portraits of Conflict…South Carolina,* 183.
193   The Miers edition incorrectly and inexplicably reads "welcome" for "wholesome."
194   Today's College Street, diagonally across Sumter Street from the LeConte's home. The festivities would have been in Emma's close proximity.

he yet seems to have some slight idea of what our feelings must be and does not vent his spite for not being received socially. Hartwell & Hatch leave today but the former leaves orders with Haughton to hold Mrs Bauskett's house and not allow her to remove anything from it. She is not even allowed to enter it. Kate has a permit from Col.Haughton "to enter her <u>father's house</u> and remove her <u>personal</u> effects." What tyranny! Col. H is distressed about it and perhaps his intercessions may finally avail to have the house restored to her.

August 6th Sunday

It has been a month since I have made an entry in this journal—But our home life is monotonous with little worth recording—And as to the condition of the country and our unhappy state as a people—it would seem better not to think of that—still less to write of it—it makes me miserable and intensifies the wicked feelings I have too much anyway. I try as hard as I can to fill my mind with other things to the exclusion of such—as far as I can I try to lose myself in books and study.

Aunt Jane and Cousin Ada[195] left Saturday (yesterday). They had received their transportation but had not expected to leave for a week or two. While at the dinner table however they suddenly received notice from Col Haughton that the wagons would leave early next morning. At eight o'clock their conveyance was at the door in the shape of a rough covered wagon—In this, after hurried adieus from all of us, they were soon seated. "Pretty rough travelling for ladies" said the Yankee who stood near assisting them. And indeed it was but they had a taste of the same kind of travelling in their Hegira from Liberty County. They hope to reach Orangeburg this afternoon where they take the cars to Charleston, thence by steamer to Savannah, arriving there probably on Wednesday—From Savannah by wagon out to the plantation. We think it rather dangerous to venture on the plantation at this season, especially as Aunt Jane is still hardly strong—It seems most unwise. We expected her to remain in Columbia until November spending the next three months with us, but as soon as she heard that Cousin Annie[196]

---

195   Joseph's sister Jane Harden and her daughter Ada.
196   Annie was Jane Harden's youngest daughter. In her memoir, Emma describes Dr. Adams in his soldier's uniform in 1862 and Cousin Annie's "raving over his good looks." Emma wrote that Annie later married Dr. Adams and lived in Augusta (22, 47).

had persisted in her resolution to accompany Dr. Adams down there she declared she must be with her and off she started. It seems a great piece of folly for Cousin Annie in her present condition to go to that debilitating climate and risk malaria but of course it is natural that her mother should feel she must be with her. They will at least be eaten up by mosquitoes. Speaking of this pest, we have scarcely felt one this summer. I wonder if it is because there are no railroads to bring them up from the coast.

Another notable event since my last entry is Miss Mary's departure for the North.[197] Her annuity has accumulated during the war and she went on about three weeks ago to see about getting it. She sent back a large part of it to Aunt Josie's family in the form of clothing. It was a sight indeed to our eyes to behold new dresses!—just to touch an organdie and silks!—The freshness of them—how really beautiful they looked! How many years it seems since we even dreamed of a new frock finer than homespun or at most calico! She had promised Sallie and me a new dress apiece but luckily I built no hopes upon her promise for I knew she would need all she had to supply Aunt Josie, so I was not disappointed, but poor Sallie was bitterly so. She had dreamed of a white dress to wear to her little dances. She sent me a white tulle bonnet trimmed with pale lilac (!) which not only goes ill with my complexion but is most strangely out of harmony with my other clothes—It will be laid aside for future consideration. Aunt Jane and cousin Ada got a new muslin apiece and father a felt hat! I was surely glad of that— for certainly his old one was most disgraceful. A new hat though looks rather odd with his old clothes. O that abominable old suit!—it hangs lankly on him, innocent of any fit and such dingy hue. His skin is tanned by exposure last winter and hair, face and garments all seem nearly the same colour. It is well a gentleman nowadays is not judged by his exterior. As for me I can get on very well through the summer if I only had a white muslin to wait on Mary Palmer in[198]—She is to be married next month and has asked me to be her bridesmaid.

---

197 Mary Graham, the unmarried sister of Aunt Josie.
198 The elder of the Rev. Dr. Benjamin M. Palmer's two daughters, Mary (1847-1925) married John Williamson Caldwell (1842-1923). Emma wrote that being bridesmaid was "my first debut into society" (Memoir, 64-67). She wondered why she was chosen because she and Mary were not particularly close.

As to how I have passed my time during the past month there is little to tell—One day is like another, but for the French one day and German the next. Kate B. asked me to read with her and I do it to oblige her feeling it a great waste of time.—It would seem I might employ the time better than going over one of my Scott's novels that I have already read.[199] But on the other hand I am too selfish anyway. Yet with studying the time that is left seems rather precious and that is why I really have dropped this diary—

Aug. 10th

Our provisional governor Perry is here[200]—Gilmore and eight other generals are here to meet him, to have a grand consultation—The town, or at least the campus, is swarming with those detestable blue coats, and negro soldiers pass and repass.

Perry has been empowered by Johnston[201] to act as he pleases with the exception of remanding the negroes to slavery. Their fine president seems disposed to adopt a conciliatory policy—Perhaps he feels a spark of attachment for the state where he once plied his trade as tailor. I believe he used to make Gov. Perry's clothes for him.[202] I am pleased to say however that South Carolina has not the honour of having given birth to this appropriate Yankee president—he is a North Carolinian.

The Convention meets in September[203]—What a contrast it will present to the one that assembled in 1860!

---

199   Sir Walter Scott, of course, one of the South's favorite novelists.
200   Benjamin F. Perry, Unionist. He served as the provisional governor, appointed by President Andrew Johnson, from late June to late November 1865. Joseph LeConte called Perry a "very dear friend, a man of noble presence, untarnished integrity, and sterling character... and the people were very well satisfied. But when the permanent government was organized in the presence of bayonets, with a carpet-bag governor, scalawag officials, and a negro legislature controlled by rascals, things became very different."
201   President Andrew Johnson.
202   Emma was accurate. Johnson did once work as a tailor in South Carolina.
203   During "Presidential Reconstruction," a convention "of the People of South Carolina" met in Columbia in September 1865, with delegates from all the districts of the state. Among other things, it repealed South Carolina's Ordinance of Secession. The *New York Times* reported on September 19, 1865, that three delegates voted "nay," and that there was "no applause" when the repeal passed. The convention of December 1860 had unanimously voted for secession.

Appendix I

Emma's aunt, Josephine LeConte, penned this powerful letter to her son about a week after the burning of Columbia. On the night of February 17th, Sherman's soldiers made several attempts to burn down her home, a fine brick house at the corner of Pendleton and Sumter streets known as the "Fourth Professor's House." Her husband John LeConte, a supervisor of the Confederate Nitre and Mining Bureau, had been ordered away, but a family friend, Dr. Carter, was with Josephine and her family, and their combined efforts saved the house from destruction.

Mrs. LeConte also informed her son about the fate of her husband and his companions, and related how some drunken Union soldiers perished by fire in a city hospital. Other Union soldiers, finding the corpses and thinking that they were dead Confederates, "severed the heads from the bodies, caught them up on their bayonets, and danced around to the tune of 'damnation to the rebels.'"

The letter is found in the LeConte Family Papers: Additions (BANC MSS C-B 1014) at the Bancroft Library at the University of California, Berkeley.

Columbia, S.C. Feb 28th '65

My own darling Boy –

Oh me! What hours of agony and suspence [*sic*] I have endured since you left me on the morning of the 15th. On the 16th your father left, in company with Capt Green and your Uncle Joe carrying with them a large amount of Baggage. I sent off every stitch of Lula's and my body clothing, all the blankets, towels, table linen sheets and your body, your brothers also, Johnnie Hardens Mitchell, Champions, Sammie Jones, and silver cups—waiters, pitchers, sugar bowls, and some silk dresses of your Aunt Jane's and Ada's, besides all my curtains and numberless other rich [racks] of value—They had not gone over 25 miles when they were overtaken by a party of Morgan's command and turned over to the provost guard of Jeff Davis Corps—Your father and brother were by the waggons [sic] keeping watch while your Uncle Joe and Capt Green were out scouting, the alarm being given your uncle and Green had time to escape but your father and brother were taken prisoners. All our effects were then broken open a bonfire made of all our clothing but the valuables were also carried off. Your father had a gun put to his breast and his watch demanded which he gave up at once, but a Capt Craft coming up took the watch from the soldier and put it in his pocket to keep for your father. The next day your brother was paroled, and allowed to come home, he brought with him a good deal of the funds belonging to the Bureau and as he was leaving the camp the officers tossed my velvet cloak to him knowing it had belonged to his family and asked him if he did not wish it. Johnnie eagerly seized it besides some daguerreotypes that belong to Mitchel or Champion.

Besides the clothes we stand in and a couple of dresses Sandy brought back for Lula are all the clothing we have in this world. The family pictures and mementoes of all sorts besides your father's books and papers and all our letters were destroyed by the burning of Dr O'Connels House. The house that covers us—a limited supply of provisions, and some funds are all that we are now worth—I will not despair if your father only returns and you can whip Sherman. London has returned—Peter and Somer were carried off—Peter told London that he should return, but Somer was so fascinated by the Gypsy life of the Army that he told London he would not come back again. It seems a Yankee fancied him and stripped a fellow to rig him up, put boots on his feet and gave him a pony and the last seen of him he was flying around in grand style.

Keep a sharp look out for Morgan's command—Jeff Davis Corps— for I feel if Peter can't get away any other way and opposing forces meet you will be sure to [meet] him. They try to console me that your father will soon be paroled but I have my doubts—They labored so [faithfully] to get your uncle and Capt Green and at times their escape was so miraculous that I fear they will visit their chagrin on him. Johnnie says they were kind to them (Dr Wallace of Columbia was caught at the same time) and treated them with every courtesy. Johnnie was as saucy as possible to them and used to answer them back on all occasions—very much to their amusement. They all called your father major from the start, seemed posted on all points which I cant help thinking very strange. One of them said to Johnnie—"The first thing you must learn to do my boy is steal." "Thank you said Johnnie none of you had to learn that for it comes very natural to you." Then the Yanks would roar with laughter and begin again at him—from his account he handled them with his gloves off.

I shall leave your father and turn now the events more closely at home—As Johnnie Harden left our door the Yanks were coming up Main Street. He could not have gone far before the stars and stripes were floating on the old State House—in a few seconds more the same thing happened to the new but what delighted my eyes was to see their battle flag blown right in two as they attempted to raise it. The wind springing up at the same time prevented their flaunting them in our faces. With effect—the whole of Logan's Corps 25 thousand men passed by our door about [4 o'clock] with their various bands of music and flags. I hardly ever saw a more hardy vigorous set of men, well clothed and fine equipments in all respects. About six in the evening their work of destruction began, the city was fired simultaneously from all points and certainly a night of more awful horrors I never passed or conceived of. About 5 in the afternoon young Sergeant [Trumbo] stopped before our gate he comforted me by telling you were still safe but that the fighting was going on and when he left shortly after Dr Carter called to give us some encouragement. We prevailed upon him to remain which he did—from that time untill he left for his native city Augusta he proved himself a most devoted friend. Nothing could surpass his generous self sacrificing care for us and to him we owe our preservation. The picture of misery and woe of our beloved city is indescribable. Nothing remains intact but the Campus grounds, Theological Seminary—the new State House, which they hadn't the powder to blow up—female college—and the Catholic church, our Episcopal church (Christ Church was burnt) the baptist, methodist and presbyterian churches—all more or less damaged and every effort made to burn them failed thro the exertions of their friends. One or two rows of buildings skirting the town are all that are left by that Vandal horde. For a long time we were in imminent danger from the flames all around us as the Piazza caught, but Dr Carter was faithful, in watching the embers and extinguishing them as they caught. To show you what villains those Yankees were they screamed out to him from the street what was he putting out the fire for? Now recollect this was from the guard that was stationed around the house to protect it. About 11 o'cl[ock] at night, there was a brigade sent to the campus to protect it. Shortly after a furious knocking at the front door tempted me to go and open. As we ladies did so, a fellow flushed with wine and every other evil passion stamped upon his face sprang in and would have immediately commenced pillage but for the ubiquitous Carter who demanded his business in such an authoritative manner that the fellow abashed at seeing a man where he only expected a number of lonely women—turned upon his heel and pretended he only came to give assistance. Carter at once ordered him to furnish it which he acquiesced in after a while by sending <u>two</u> men ...

[several sentences and words here and below are illegible because of stains and tears in the paper]

The night seemed endless as we struggled against the fiery embers, while on the street below a throng of vengeful bluecoats appeared to rejoice in the travail. As each house was enveloped in flames their demoniac yells of delight coupled with with [*sic*] the shrieks and screams of widdows [*sic*] and orphans who sought the [lawn for asylum] in front of our house for protection beggars description. All night long from the Piazza and roof the women fought the flames and there were times when the panes of glass were so hot that you could not rest your hand there for any time but still we fought—and there stood that sea of upturned faces of Logan's Corps with not one spark of sympathy for us. [There was no light or water on the] campus for the first thing these devils did was to blow up the gas and destroy the waterworks—we were absolutely in their power and bitterly did we grieve over it. At daylight the flames began to subside and I threw myself upon the bed to rest when tramp, tramp, tramp, resounded through the house, upon rising, found that half doz[en] fellows had entered the house from the Kitchen declaring the house was on fire rushed up to the garret pretending to put out the fire—when lo and behold they tore up the tin and deliberately set my house afire———

As the main army was about moving off they sent the provost guard to encamped [*sic*] just in front of my house. The officer in command Major Seay of Iowa and staff—rode up to our front gate to know if they could obtain quarters. Dr Carter suggested it would secure further molestation if we took some of them in. I cannot say they were gentlemen but they certainly treated us with every courtesy by not intruding upon our privacy. We were in great terror lest when the main army disappeared we should be burnt out by the stragglers who had vowed vengeance against our house and the college buildings. Our house they seemed to have a particular spite against us for no other reason that I can now see but that we kept so within doors and with every door and blind shut tight—they thought this defiant and of course were itching to get at the inside of it. They took nothing from your father's library nor disturbed the books if I except the bottle of ink. They however left their names and command written upon the wall in a conspicuous place <u>there</u> they <u>shall</u> <u>remain</u> as long as I live here.

About 11 on Sunday morning after that awful night they brought all the combustible materials for burning the college but by the prompt measures of Dr Thompson who denounced them and the active measures of the commanding Generals the buildings were saved, not however before some of the torch bearers tasted of cold steel. I am sure it was the presence of <u>their</u> own men in our Hospital that saved it nothing else.

They burned the Ladies Hospital—fortunately all the sick were removed to our Hospital during the day except the corpse of one man. During the carnival of death and destruction a number of their own men sought a bed there as their beastly intoxication could carry them no farther—these were burned up—As the flames progressed they could be seen tearing their hair and screaming for help—but help there was none—and when the building fell in they all perished. Instantly the yells of delight filled the air, frantically they advanced severed the heads from the bodies, caught them up on their bayonets, and danced around to the tune of "damnation to the rebels" little dreaming that they were their own men. Our ladies were insulted on all sides by vile language, but I have not heard of any violations—the negro element surpassed itself for outlawry, billets of burning wood would be thrown at their heads and every species of insulting language use to their owners—immense droves of them left with army—many families were left without one, and all now doing all their work—Annie and Bobbie remained faithful among the faithless in fact she has helped to feed us from the plunder acquired when the stores were thrown open. [Bessie's] all intended to leave, but finding the army could not furnish waggons for them to ride in concluded to remain. [Mag] and Adams were burnt out—they also left with army besides thousands of other white people—You wonder as you pick your way through the ruins what has become of the people and where have they gone to? You can walk miles about our city and never meet a soul the sense of loneliness and desolation is intolerable. I am about writing to all my friends for help in the way of food. I have enough for present purposes but we must look ahead—fortunately we have funds enough on hand to help us along for some time. If your father were only back I should cease to grieve—but let us ... [Your uncle Joseph is home] and will shortly go down to the Manning settlement for supplies, after that they propose going to Augusta that is Capt Green and himself—to procure some clothing. Capt Green and his wife are staying with us it adds to my cares but security also.

The Gibbes were burnt out—didn't save a second stitch of clothing, this is the fate of <u>all</u> our friends. Do let us hear from you every opportunity that offers no matter how few the lines they will be a comfort to my heart. God bless you! My own precious boy and when the opportunity offers strike a blow that that accursed race shall feel in defense for your desolated home and unhappy mother.

Appendix II

EMMA'S COUSIN MARY TALLULAH ("Lula") LeConte wrote this letter to Captain J. W. Walker, who was probably a family friend. The letter is part of the LeConte Family Papers: Additions (BANC MSS 70/24 c) at the Bancroft Library, University of California, Berkeley.

> *Columbia, S.C.*
> *Feb. 28th 1865*

According to the promise made to you on the eve of your departure, I now write to you, by the first opportunity going northwards, in order to inform you in some faint degree of what has transpired since we parted. The last three weeks have been so crowded with events that an attempt at retrospection bewilders me, and I scarce know where to begin. Sherman's army, after its departure from Savannah, advanced with its characteristic celerity and was within a few miles of Branchville before our generals deemed to have any distinct idea of his whereabouts. Finding that in all probability we would make a stand at Branchville, Sherman executed one of his oft-repeated manouvres [*sic*], flanked Branchville and advanced rapidly on Columbia. When it became evident that Columbia would be attacked, the generals supposing it would be only by a part of Sherman's force, sent a few reinforcements here, among which was the Chatham Artillery, and for a few days Jule was with us nearly all the time as he was the only one in the company from Columbia, and the Captain allowed him many privileges. We had expected to leave with Papa when he left, but the authorities spoke confidently of holding the city, and advised him to delay taking off the government property. You may judge of the ignorance in which we were kept when I tell you the city was surrendered on Friday at 11 o'clock and Papa only left on Thursday at daylight. We had at that time arrived at the conclusion that we would stay and take the consequences. At the eleventh hour Gen. Beauregard discovered that the whole of Sherman's army was engaged in the attack, and it was useless attempting to hold the place. All of Thursday the 15th the enemy shelled the town, however doing no damage although fragments fell in every direction, and I have preserved some mementoes of the Yankees in some pieces which fell in our yard. Thursday night and Friday morning our forces were withdrawing from the town, and at 11 o'clock it was surrendered. Jule had been engaged in the fight all the day before, and although we heard of his safety, he was obliged to leave without our seeing him, and since then we have heard nothing of him. Johnnie Harden, being mounted, left the company and stopped for a moment to see us. We filled his knapsack, and he dashed off from our door at full speed just as the Yankee yells were heard advancing down Main St., not five minutes after the hated stars and stripes ran up in triumph over the state-house. I turned from the window where I was standing with a feeling of intense loathing hatred; my father and brothers fugitives from their own home, and the emblem of Yankee triumph flaunting in our faces; there are some things very hard to bear. As soon as the Army entered the town Dr Thompson, head surgeon at the Hospital demanded a guard, and our house being within the Campus enclosure, we, in about fifteen or twenty minutes, had an armed Yankee walking his beat in front of our door. About four in the afternoon the column of 25,000 began passing our house to their encampment. They were a fine looking body of men, splendidly armed and equipped, and seemingly under perfect discipline. Friday night, what a night of horrors it was. As soon as the Yankees entered the town we noticed columns of smoke rising in different directions, but did not pay much attention to it thinking our own forces were burning cotton as they retreated. The mayor, upon Sherman's arrival in town, had gone to him to know what we had to expect from his troops that night, and with usual perfidy Sherman told him to let the people rest in peace, they had nothing to fear. The wind had been blowing heavily all day and steadily increased after sundown; about nine o'clock the fires began to break out in every direction, and soon the whole of Main Street was in a blaze. As night advanced the flames raged yet more wildly and were spreading to an alarming extent in our portion of the town, and yet there was not the slightest effort upon the part of the Yankee generals to restrain the troops. The water had all been cut off and there was nothing to check the flames. Meanwhile, as the flames rushed angrily on carrying every thing before them and while thousands of defenceless women & children were running wildly weeping through the streets, having saved nothing but the clothes upon them, these creatures calling themselves men stood idly by, laughingly exulting in the misery and desolation they had created. Still the fires spread, the State House caught and the flames rushed heaven-high; this I had expected and did not regret, for after having been polluted by having the stars and stripes float over it, I think I myself would have applied the torch if Yankee malice had spared it. The fire still spread fearfully and we began to fear for our own safety. All the houses in the neighbourhood were in a blaze, and while we stood at the windows, on the roof brushing off the sparks, we saw the torch applied to the houses across the street, and now began our struggle for a roof to shelter us; we dared not open the door to ask for assistance, as hundreds of infuriated demons were without ready to rush in, sack and pillage. The wood-work about the house caught fire several times, but owing to the fact that the roof was tin, we, together with Dr Carter of Augusta whose superhuman efforts in aiding and protecting us we can never forget, were able to keep the fire under until all immediate danger was past. Saturday morning dawned bright and beautiful; the flames were dying sullenly away, more from a want of material to consume than any other reason, and by the fresh morning light we looked into each others pale careworn, exhausted faces, and felt that in saving our home we were immeasurably more blest than thousands in our own town. You would not recognize our once beautiful town in the mass of ruins which now greets your eye on every side; scarcely a fourth of it now remains. The Yankee generals are now somewhat ashamed of their own conduct, and try to excuse it by saying the troops were drunk and uncontrollable, which is all nonsense and false as they are themselves; however, "to give the devil his due," towards daylight there did seem to be some slight attempt to keep the Hospital from taking fire, and a detachment of men was placed at our back gate. But I believe the destruction of the town was premeditated and intentional; the soldiery went too systematically to work, there was too much "method in their madness" to attribute to drunken fury. All of Saturday and Saturday night they were very quiet; we were not disturbed at all; on Sunday morning the provost or rear guard of the Army encamped on the green in front of our house, and the Lt. Col commanding took up his quarters with us. Although a Yankee I shall always bear testimony of his gentlemanly conduct. He merely occupied the Library and did not take even his meals with us, never intruded on the family, and altogether showed a consideration and delicacy which I had not expected & for which I shall always feel deeply grateful to Col. Seay. On Monday morning the Army moved out, but we were not molested at all; in fact our house was not entered at all during their stay. I never saw a Yankee face to face or exchanged a syllable with them. Mama had of course to receive the Col. and give him his apartment, but I kept above stairs. Dr. Carter, who was stationed at the Hospital here, stayed with us all the time, assisted us in every way in his power, and I feel we can never sufficiently repay his self-sacrificing kindness. We have all been so much pleased with him, that Mama wants you to tell us all about him, whom he married &c &c; she knew his mother well in days gone by, and therefore feels a two-fold interest in him.

And now I have yet more of our trials to tell you. Papa left home, as I before mentioned, on Thursday morning in company with Uncle Joe, Johnnie, and Capt Green. They travelled on rather slowly with the wagons, and on Saturday morning, to their dismay, found themselves surrounded by the enemy; they lay concealed in the woods all Saturday, and Saturday night; early on Sunday morning about seven o'clock, Uncle Joe and the Capt went out to scout. They had only been gone a few moments, when the enemy, led by a negro, surrounded the camp, rushed upon Papa and Johnnie, and captured them ere they had time to attempt an escape. Johnnie remained a prisoner with Papa a day and night, when the Captain of the Provost Guard, in consideration of his youth and delicate condition, for he had just recovered from an attack of measles, furnished him with a pass, and he walked all the way home. Papa is still a prisoner in their hands. If I could only think he would be paroled, or could ever hear something definite from him the suspense would not be so terrible. I try to bear up and be cheerful on Mama's account, for she is so sad, but there are times when I am heart-sick with misery at the thought of how long a time may elapse before we see Papa again. Papa a prisoner, and Jule so situated that we are unable to hear from him, the future does indeed seem a blank. I neglected to mention that Uncle Joe and Capt Green, after skulking in the woods for several days, and making numerous hair-breadths escapes, have finally reached home safely.

At the same time that Papa was captured, the Yankees took the trunks containing all our wearing apparel which we had sent off with him for safety. After ransacking the trunks, and taking whatever pleased their fancy, these instruments of Sherman's destructive policy, applied the torch, and burned the remainder. We are now left with merely the change we retained at home. But I will not write any longer on the topic of our losses.

Johnnie says I must tell you he is going to write to Augusta for your gun, which you kindly offered to lend him when you were last here, and hopes you will have no objection. The Yankees took all his fire-arms when he was captured, and shooting is his only amusement now. He will take good care of it and your mother is not to send it unless she finds a good opportunity coming to Columbia.

Aunt Jane and Ada are now with us, and have been for some time past. We are very glad to have them, for during Papa's absence their presence will be a comfort to all of us.

I hope you will write soon, and as often as you hear of couriers coming this way. Mama sends her love to you.

Sincerely your friend,
Lula LeConte
Capt. J. W. Walker

Appendix III

FAMILY CONNECTIONS

The Children of Louis Leconte (1783-1838) & Anne Quarterman Leconte (1793-1826)

1. William LeConte (1812-1841) m. Sarah Nisbet (Aunt Sallie)

   a. James Nisbet ("Jimmer") (1834-1863)
   b. Anne (1836-1922) m. Clifford Anderson
   c. William Louis (1838-1866)
   d. Sarah Ophelia (1841-1878)

2. Jane LeConte (1813-1876)

   m. John McPherson Berrien Harden (1810-1848)

   a. Matilda Jane ("Cousin Tillie," 1837-1932) m. Thomas Sumner b. Stevens (1820-1889), daughter, Anne Rosa Stevens Ramsey (1862-1958)
   c. John Le Conte Harden ("Cousin Johnny," 1839-1902)
   d. Ada Louisa Harden ("Cousin Ada," (1845-1930))
   e. Annie m. Dr. Adams

3. John Eaton LeConte (1818-1891)

   m. Eleanor Josephine Graham ("Aunt Josie") (1824-1894)

   a. Mary Tallulah LeConte "Lula" (1843-1868)
   b. Louis Julian ("Jule" or "Jules," 1845-1920)
   c. John Cecil ("Cousin Johnnie," 1850-1874)

4. Louis Eaton LeConte, Sr. (1821-1851)

   m. Harriet Nisbet ("Aunt Harriet") (1824-1892)

   a. Eva Harriet (1844-1911)
   b. William ("Cousin Willie," (1846-1875)
   c. John Nisbet (1848-1925)
   d. Louis Eaton, Jr. ("Cousin Louis," 1849-1883)
      m. Caroline Hopkins Adams

5. Joseph Quarterman LeConte (1823-1901)

   m. Caroline Elizabeth Nisbet ("Bessie") (1828-1915)

      a. Emma Florence (1847-1932) m. Farish Carter Furman (1846-1883)
      b. Sarah ("Sallie," 1850-1915) m. Robert Means Davis (1840-1904)
      c. Josephine Eloise ("Little Josie," 1859-1861)
      d. Caroline Eaton ("Carrie," 1863-1945)
      e. Joseph Nisbet (1870-1950)

6. Anne LeConte (1825-1866)

   m. Josiah Peter Stevens (1818-1897)

      a. Ella Florine (1845-1914)
      b. Walter LeConte ("Cousin Walter," 1847-1927)
      c. Josiah Percival ("Cousin Percy," 1852-1929)
         m. Jeannie Alexander (1855-1950)
      d. Anna Louisa (1860-1867)
      e. Mabel Caroline (1862-1874)

The Children Of Alfred Moore Nisbet (1797-1875) & Sarah Stillwell Nisbet (1795-1868)

1. Caroline Elizabeth (1828-1915) (Emma LeConte's mother)

2. Sarah Angelina ("Aunt Sallie," 1834-1911)

   m. Alexander Moffett (1832-1899)

3. Emily Hines (1832-1905) m. Benjamin Mitchell Polhill

4. Mary Ophelia (died young)

5. Edwin Alfred (1831-1901) m. Henrietta Waters (1845-1907)

5. Joseph Henry (1825-1890) m. Emmie D. DeLauney (1830-1896)

ILLUSTRATIONS

Emma's page one of her recopied diary of the 1870s.
Digital Southern Historical Collection, UNC.

Emma Florence LeConte

The photograph of Emma pictures the long braided hair she describes being popular with her beaux. (Mentioned in Introduction).

*Joseph LeConte, Emma's father, around 1860,
from a painting by William Scarborough.*

Photograph of Joseph LeConte by Quinby of Charleston, S.C.

Photograph of John LeConte, circa 1865.

Josephine LeConte, Emma's "Aunt Josie," photographed in 1850.
Bancroft Library, University of California-Berkeley.

Caroline Elizabeth Nisbet
("Bessie")

Sarah LeConte
("Sallie," 1850-1915)

Caroline Eaton LeConte
("Carrie" 1863-1945).

"View of Sidney Park from the John Taylor House" by Augustus Grinevald, ca. 1859. A watercolour painting of the beautiful city of Columbia. Courtesy of the South Caroliniana Library, University of South Carolina, Columbia, S.C.

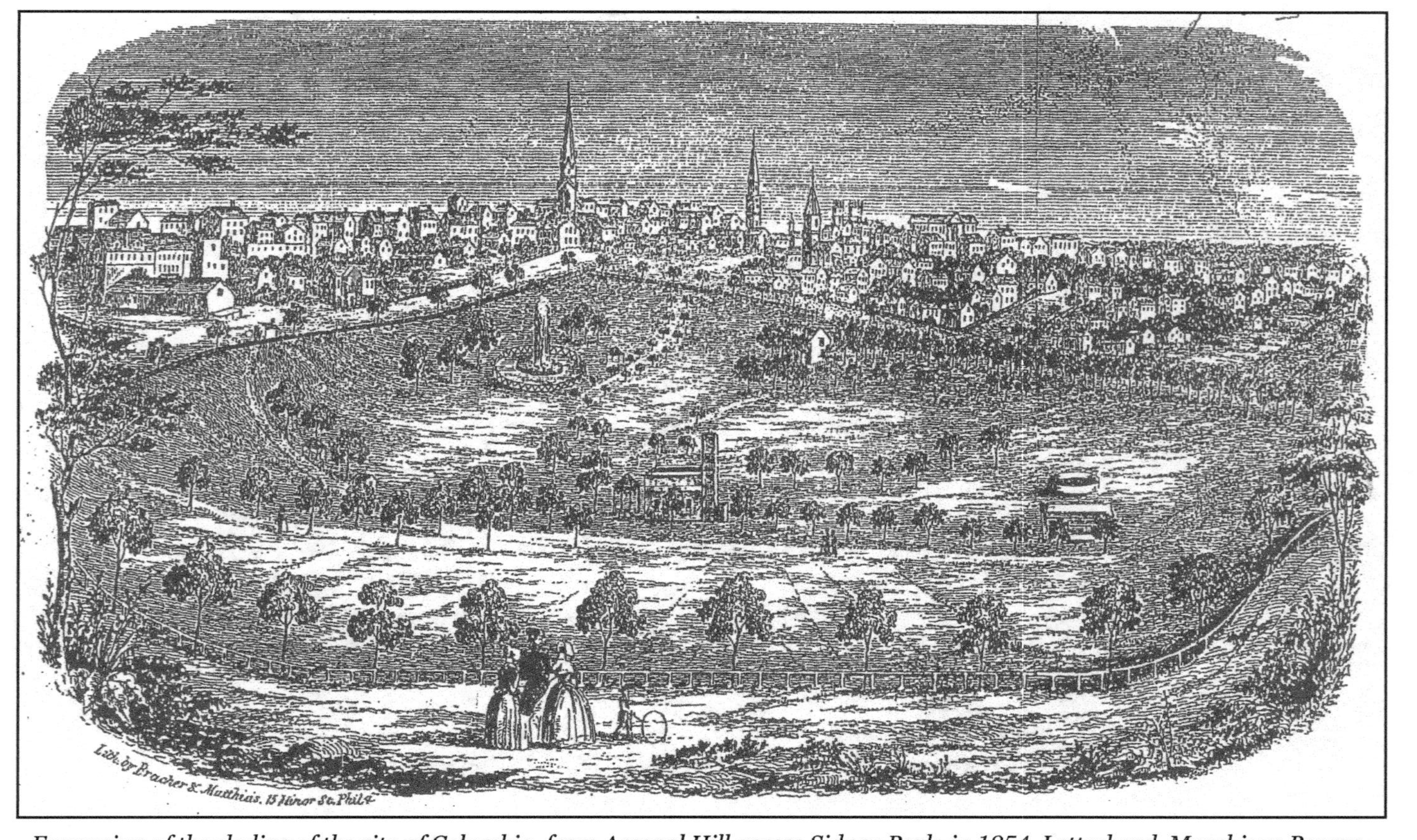

Engraving of the skyline of the city of Columbia, from Arsenal Hill across Sidney Park, in 1854. Letterhead, Murchison Papers. Courtesy of the South Caroliniana Library, University of South Carolina, Columbia, S.C.

The city of Columbia from across the Congaree River, as depicted in New York Illustrated News, 6 January 1861, from a sketch by Hugo Bosse.

The campus of South Carolina College around 1850, lithograph by C. B. Graham from a painting by Eugene A. D'Ovilliers. The new college library with its white columns is shown at the front far left. The LeContes lived directly across the green from it at the front far right.

*Detail of the LeContes' "Third Professor's House," now Lieber College.
Emma's room was the second floor's two right windows.
Note the ivy growing at her window sills as she described in her diary.*

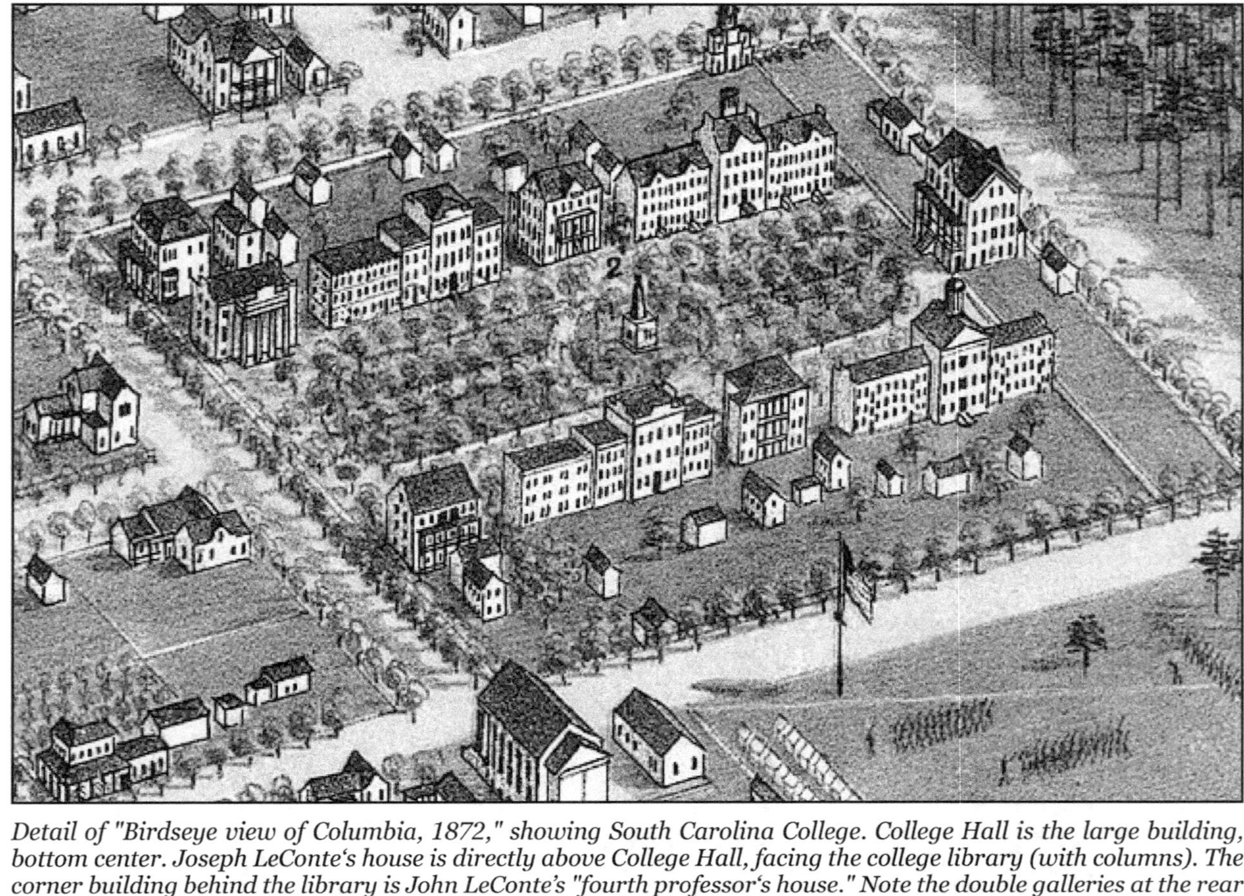

Detail of "Birdseye view of Columbia, 1872," showing South Carolina College. College Hall is the large building, bottom center. Joseph LeConte's house is directly above College Hall, facing the college library (with columns). The corner building behind the library is John LeConte's "fourth professor's house." Note the double galleries at the rear of Joseph LeConte's house, as Emma described in her diary. Courtesy of LOC.

The Fourth Professor's House, South Carolina College, around 1910. Built in 1859 for John and Josie LeConte and their family. Courtesy of the South Caroliniana Library, University of South Carolina, Columbia, S.C.

College Hall, constructed on the campus in 1859 south of the LeConte's home, and where Emma described Col. Haughton making his "wholesome" speech to the freedmen. The photograph dates to around 1875.

Engraving, ca. 1880, of Columbia Female Academy, where Emma had classes. Plain (later Hampton) Street, designed by George E. Walker and constructed in 1859.

Eyewitness sketch of General Sherman's army crossing the Congaree River into Columbia on 17 February 1865, in Harper's Weekly.

*The entry of Sherman and his command into the city,
17 February 1865.* Harper's Weekly, *1 April 1865.*

William Waud's eyewitness sketch of the burning of Columbia,
Harper's Weekly, *8 April 1865.*

The ruins of General Wade Hampton's Millwood Plantation in 1905. From the original edition of Mary Chesnut's A Diary from Dixie.

Occupation of the Hampton-Preston Mansion on Blanding Street by U.S. General John A. Logan. Harper's Weekly, *15 April 1865. The house escaped burning through the shrewd action of Sister Baptista Lynch. Logan was known to be Sherman's most destructive officer, and was sent into the city with his 15th Corps.*

*A view of the garden of the Hampton-Preston Mansion with a U.S. soldier.*Harper's Weekly, *15 April 1865.*

The Hampton-Preston Mansion in January 1996.
Clint Kastner photographer.

The 18th Iowa Regiment of the 17th U.S. Army Corps raising the U.S. flag over the new State House. An eyewitness sketch by J.E. Taylor published in Frank Leslie's Illustrated Magazine, *8 April 1865.*

The old 18th century South Carolina State House as pictured in
Frank Leslie's Illustrated News, *17 August 1861.*

*Raising the U.S. flag over the old State House. An eyewitness sketch
by Theodore Davis from* Harper's Weekly, *21 July 1865.*

Ruins of the old State House. Harper's Weekly, 1 April 1865. Lost in the destruction was the legislative library and valuable state archives.

Ruins of Richland District Court House at rear, as seen through another fire-gutted public building. Photo by George Barnard, June 1866. National Archive.

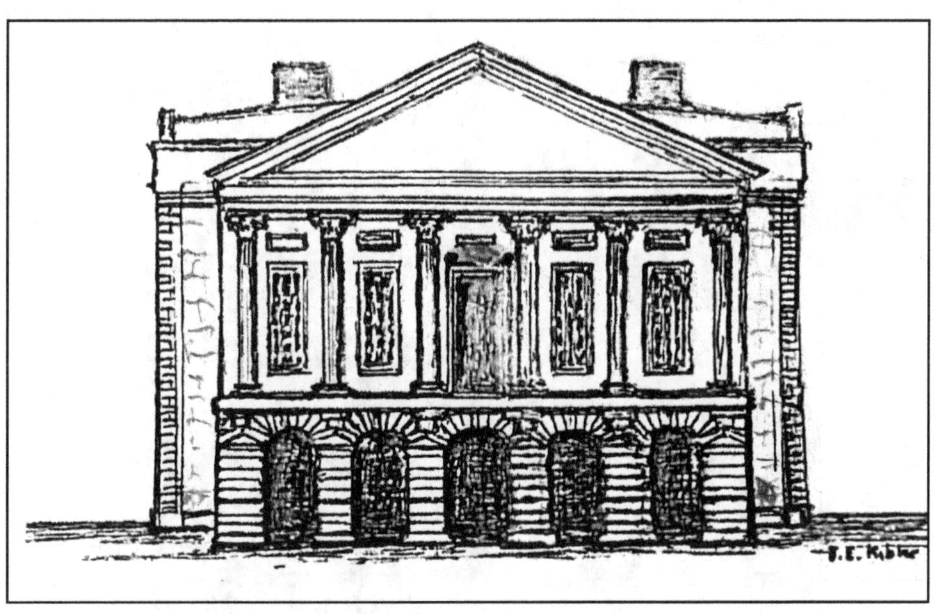

Image of the Richland District Court House reconstructed from photos of its ruins. Built in 1858 from a design by George E. Walker. The elegant neo-Roman structure featured fluted granite columns of single shafts. Mixed Media, J.E. Kibler, 2017.

Columbia's main street looking north from the State House grounds, May–June 1865, photographed by Richard Wearn. As Emma said, when she walked across the city to Arsenal Hill, she passed through many blocks of ashes and crumbling chimneys.

Columbia City Hall and clock tower. A rare engraving from around 1864-1865.

Sketch of the ruins of Columbia's main street, Frank Leslie's Illustrated News, 8 April 1865

Sketch of the ruins of Columbia looking north from the State House, by Theodore Davis, Harper's Weekly, 21 July 1865.

*Ruins of the Ursuline Convent
photographed by Richard Wearn, May-June 1865.*

*Ruins of Washington Street Methodist Church,
photographed by Richard Wearn, May-June 1865.*

Rear view of Christ Episcopal Church, Blanding Street, photographed by Richard Wearn, May–June 1865.

Reconstructed rear of Christ Episcopal Church, mixed media, James E. Kibler, Jr., 2017. Christ Church was designed by Columbia's first master architect, George Edward Walker around 1858 in the Neo Gothic style that was popular for Anglican church architecture at the time. Its large sanctuary seated six hundred.

Reconstructed front view of Christ Episcopal Church, photographed by Richard Wearn, May-June 1865. Mixed media by James E. Kibler, Jr., 2017. Emma's descriptions of the church ruins are particularly evocative.

*The Presbyterian Lecture Rooms ruins, designed by George Edward Walker.
Photograph by Richard Wearn, May-June 1865.*

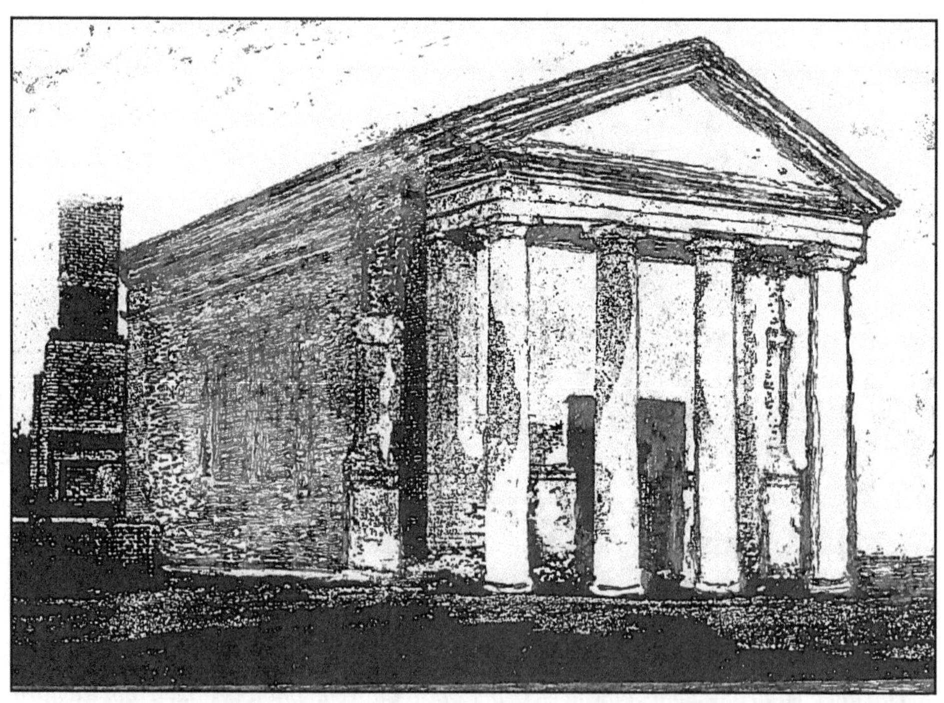

Reconstructed Lecture Rooms, mixed media, James E. Kibler, Jr., 2017.

Ruins of the Dr. Robert W. Gibbes Mansion, photographed by by Richard Wearn, May-June 1865. Dr. Gibbes was a friend and scientific colleague of the LeConte brothers. Here he lost his scientific collections by which he was formulating a theory of evolution a decade before Charles Darwin. Note the large walled garden and dead or recovering street trees.

Ruins of the Thomas B. Clarkson Mansion, corner Blanding and Bull, which was built by James Henry Hammond in 1836. Photograph by Richard Wearn, May-June 1865. The building, with tall granite Corinthian columns on all four sides, was one of America's finest Roman Revival homes. Hammond modeled the house after a dwelling he saw in Rome. The Clarksons had several sons in the Confederate Army, and the house was thus a special target for destruction.

Ruins of the city jail on Washington Street. Photograph by Richard Wearn, May-June 1865.

138

Eyewitness sketch of life among the ruins of Columbia by Theodore Davis, Harper's Weekly, *21 July 1865. This image corroborates Emma's description.*

Works Cited

A Guide to Confederate Columbia. Tuscaloosa, AL: Mary Noel Kershaw Foundation, 1996.

Allston, Robert F. W. *The South Carolina Rice Plantation as Revealed in the Papers of Robert F. W. Allston*. Edited by. J. H. Easterby. Chicago, IL: University of Chicago Press, 1945.

Anderson, Richard LeConte. *LeConte History and Genealogy, Vol. II*. Macon, GA: Richard Anderson, 1981.

Brady, Lisa M. *War upon the Land*. Athens: University of Georgia Press, 2012.

Byers, Samuel H. M. "The Burning of Columbia." *Lippincott's Magazine* (March 1882).

Carlisle, Catherine A. "Translating the Landscape: Eugene D'ovilliers and Landscape Painting in the South" Master's Thesis, University of NC, Chapel Hill, NC, 2014.

Chesnut, Mary Boykin. *Mary Chesnut's Civil War*. Edited by C. Vann Woodward. New Haven, CT: Yale University Press, 1981.

Chesnut, Mary Boykin. *Mary Chesnut's Diary from Dixie*. Edited by Isabella Martin. The Mulberry Edition, Vol. I. Gretna, LA: Pelican, 2011.

Chesnut, Mary Boykin. *Mary Chesnut's Civil War Photograph Album*. Edited by Martha M. Daniels and Barbara McCarthy. The Mulberry Edition, Vol. II. Gretna, LA: Pelican, 2011.

Cisco, Walter Brian. *War Crimes Against Southern Civilians*. Gretna, LA: Pelican, 2007.

Conrad, August. *The Destruction of Columbia, S.C.* Roanoke, VA: Stone Printing, 1902.

Conyngham, David P. *General Sherman's March Through the South.* New York: Sheldon, 1865.

Culpepper, Marilyn Mayer. *Women of the Civil War South.* Jefferson, NC: McFarland and Co., 2004.

DiLorenzo, Thomas. *The Problem with Lincoln.* Washington, D.C.: Regnery History, 2020.

Elmore, Tom. *A Carnival of Destruction: Sherman's Invasion of South Carolina.* Charleston, SC: Joggling Board Press, 2012.

Emerson, Eric, and Karen Stokes, eds. *Days of Destruction: Augustine Smythe and the Civil War Siege of Charleston.* Columbia: University of South Carolina Press, 2017.

Gibbes, James Guignard. *Who Burnt Columbia?* Newberry, SC: Elbert Aull, 1902.

Gibbes, Robert W., Jr. *The Present Earth: The Remains of a Former World.* Columbia, SC: A. S. Johnston, 1849.

Gibbes, Robert W., Jr. *A Memoir of James De Veaux.* Edited by Alexander Moore. Columbia: University of South Carolina Press, 2012.

Gibbes, Robert W., Jr. *Cuba for Invalids.* New York: Townsend, 1860.

Green, Anna Maria. *The Journal of a Milledgeville Girl, 1861-1867.* Edited by James C. Bonner. Athens: University of Georgia Press, 1964.

Gregg, Maxcy. *Maxcy Gregg's Sporting Journals, 1842-1858.* Edited by Suzanne Parfitt Johnson. Columbia, SC: Green Altar Books, 2017.

Graydon, Nell S. *Tales of Columbia.* Columbia, SC: R. L. Bryan, 1964.

Hogan, Edward R. *Of the Human Heart: A Biography of Benjamin Peirce.* Bethlehem, PA: Lehigh University Press, 2008.

Hollis, Daniel Walker. *University of South Carolina. South Carolina College,* Vol. I. Columbia: University of South Carolina Press, 1951.

Howard, Oliver Otis. *Autobiography,* Vol. II. New York: Taylor, 1908.

Huger, Alfred. "The Burning of Columbia." *New York World* (August 1866).

Kibler, James E., Jr. *Poems from Scorched Earth*. Charleston, SC: Charleston Press, 2000.

Kibler, James E., Jr. *The Classical Origins of Southern Literature* (2nd Ed.). McClellanville, SC: Abbeville Institute Press, 2023.

Kibler, James E., Jr. "Simms's Editorship of the *Columbia Phoenix* of 1865," *South Carolina Journals and Journalists*. Edited by James B. Meriwether. Columbia, SC: Southern Studies Program, 1975, 61-75.

Kibler, James E., Jr. "Antebellum Ghost Gardens." *Columbia Metropolitan Magazine* (May 2019), 100-106.

Kibler, James E., Jr. "Columbia's First Master Architect [George Edward Walker]." *Columbia Metropolitan Magazine* (November 2019), 42-48.

Kibler, James E., Jr. "The Silver Lining. Bringing Columbia Heirlooms Back Home." *Columbia Metropolitan Magazine* (March 2020), 51-56.

Lawton, Cecilia. *Incidents in the Life of Cecilia Lawton*. Edited by Karen Stokes. Macon, GA: Mercer University Press, 2021.

LeConte, Caroline. "An Introductory Reminiscence" in Joseph Le Conte, *'Ware Sherman*, xv-xxi.

LeConte, Emma. *When the Worled Ended: The Diary of Emma Le Conte*. Edited by Earl Schenck Miers. New York: Oxford University Press, 1957; paperback edition, Lincoln: University of Nebraska Press, 1987, foreword by Anne Firor Scott.

LeConte, Emma. "Reminiscence of Emma Le Conte Furman." Unpublished manuscript, 1931. Emma Talley Shaw Collection, Hargrett Library, University of Georgia.

LeConte, John (of Philadelphia). "Southern Plants Worthy of Cultivation," *The Florist and Horticultural Journal* (Philadelphia), II (November 1853), 333-334. William Summer's copy in the collection of J.E. Kibler.

LeConte, Joseph. *Religion and Science*. New York: Appleton, 1873.

LeConte, Joseph. *The Autobiography of Joseph LeConte*. Edited by William Dallam Armes. New York: Appleton, 1903.

LeConte, Joseph. *'Ware Sherman: A Journal of Three Months' Personal Experience in the Last Days of the Confederacy*. Berkeley: University of California, 1937.

McCaslin, Richard B. *Portraits of Conflict: A Photographic History of South Carolina in the Civil War*. Fayetteville: University of Arkansas Press, 1994.

McCord, Louisa S. *Poems, Drama, Biography, Letters*. Edited by Richard C. Lounsbury. Charlottesville: University Press of Virginia, 1996.

McNeely, Patricia. *Sherman's Flame and Blame Campaign*. Columbia, S C: Pat McNeely, 2018.

Moore, John Hammond. *Columbia and Richland County*. Columbia: University of South Carolina Press, 1993.

Nichols, George Ward. *The Story of the Great March*. New York: Harper, 1865.

Nicholson, William A. *The Burning of Columbia*. Columbia, SC: Williams, Sloan, 1895.

Pinckney, C. C., Peter J. Shand, and Paul Trapier. *Report of the Committee on the Destruction of Churches in the Diocese of South Carolina, During the Late War, Presented to the Protestant Episcopal Convention, May, 1868*. Charleston, SC: Walker, Agt. Stationer and Printer, 1868.

Pringle, Elizabeth W. Allston. *Chronicles of "Chicora Wood."* New York: Scribner's, 1922.

Ruffin, Edmund. *Incidents of My Life. Edmund Ruffin's Autobiographical Essays*. Charlottesville: University Press of Virginia, 1990.

Ruffin, Edmund. *Agriculture, Geology, and Society in Antebellum South Carolina. The Private Diary of Edmund Ruffin, 1843*. Athens: University of Georgia Press, 1992.

Scott, Edwin J., *Random Recollections of a Long Life, 1806-1876*. Columbia, SC: Charles A. Calvo, Jr., 1884.

Simms, William Gilmore. *The Letters of William Gilmore Simms*, Volume IV. Columbia: University of South Carolina Press, 1955.

Simms, William Gilmore. *Sack and Destruction of the City of Columbia, S. C.*, ed. Alexander S. Salley. Freeport, NY: Books for Libraries Press, 1971.

Simms, William Gilmore. *A City Laid Waste*. Edited by David Aiken. Columbia: University of South Carolina Press, 2005.

Stephens, Lester D. *Joseph Le Conte: Gentle Prophet of Evolution*. Baton Rouge: LSU Press, 1982.

Stephens, Lester D. *Science, Race, and Religion in the American South: John Bachman and the Charleston Circle of Naturalists, 1815-1895*. Chapel Hill: University of North Carolina Press, 2000.

Stokes, Karen. *South Carolina Civilians in Sherman's Path*. Charleston, SC: The History Press, 2012.

Stokes, Karen. *Confederate South Carolina: True Stories of Civilians, Soldiers and the War*. Charleston, SC: The History Press, 2015.

Stokes, Karen. *A Legion of Devils: Sherman in South Carolina*. Columbia, SC: Shotwell Publishing, 2017.

Stokes, Karen. "Northern Lies about the Burning of Columbia." Abbeville Institute. *Abbeville Blog* (15 February 2018).

Taylor, Mrs. Thomas, Mrs. Augustine T. Smythe, et al, eds. *South Carolina Women in the Confederacy*. Columbia, S C: State Company, 1903.

Trezevant, Dr. D. H. *The Burning of Columbia, S. C.* Columbia: South Carolinian Power Press, 1866.

Wright, Henry H. *A History of the Sixth Iowa Infantry*. Iowa City: State Historical Society, 1923.

Wright, Henry H. "The Awfullest Time I Ever Seen." *Civil War History,* 8 (September 1962).

INDEX

About the Editors

JAMES KIBLER was born in Prosperity, South Carolina and graduated from the University of South Carolina with a Ph.D. in English. His interests have lead him to write on diverse subjects, from botany and agriculture to architecture and art. As a literary man, he has written in several genres, including the novel, short story, and poetry. The history and saga of the renovation of his plantation house is chronicled in his critically acclaimed *Our Fathers' Fields*, which was awarded the prestigious Fellowship of Southern Writers Award for Nonfiction.

It is rare for a writer to excel as both a creative artist and a scholar, but Kibler has achieved such distinction. For many years he was Professor of English at the University of Georgia, he has written authoritatively on many aspects of Southern literature. As a scholar, Kibler is largely responsible for the contemporary rise of William Gilmore Simms studies. He is the founding editor of *Simms Review*, author of the definitive work on Simms's poetry, and the discoverer of many previously unknown Simms writings. His *Faulkner the Southerner and The Classical Origins of Southern Literature* (New and Enlarged Second Edition) were published in 2023. His most recent works are the novel *The Gentler Gamester*, published in 2024, and *Beyond the Stone: Poems of Tribute & Remembrance*, published in 2025.

KAREN STOKES, an archivist at the South Carolina Historical Society in Charleston, is the prolific author of over a dozen history books about South Carolina and its people during the War Between the States, all based on primary manuscript sources. These include, among others, *South Carolina Civilians in Sherman's Path, The Immortal 600, A Confederate Englishman, Confederate South Carolina, Days of Destruction, A Legion of Devils: Sherman in South Carolina, Fortunes of War: The Adventures of a German Confederate, Carolina Love Letters*, and *A Confederate in Paris: Letters of A. Dudley Mann 1867-1879*. She has also written works of historical fiction published by Green Altar (an imprint of Shotwell Publishing) including *Belles, The Immortals*, and *Honor in the Dust*.

Green Altar (Literary Imprint)

CATHARINE SAVAGE BROSMAN
An Aesthetic Education and Other Stories (2nd Ed)

Chained Tree, Chained Owls: Poems

Aerosols and Other Poems

Partial Memoirs

RANDALL IVEY
*A New England Romance:
and Other Southern Stories*

The Gift of Gab

SUZANNE JOHNSON
Maxcy Gregg's Sporting Journals 1842–1858

JAMES E. KIBLER, JR.
Tiller: Claybank County Series, Vol. 4

The Gentler Gamester

*Beyond The Stone: Poems of
Tribute & Remembrance*

THOMAS MOORE
*A Fatal Mercy:
The Man Who Lost The Civil War*

PERRIN LOVETT
The Substitute, Tom Ironsides 1

Judging Athena

KAREN STOKES
Belles
Carolina Twilight
Honor in the Dust
The Immortals
The Soldier's Ghost: A Tale of Charleston

WILLIAM THOMAS
*Runaway Haley:
An Imagined Family Saga*

*The Field of Justice: Moonshine
and Murder in North Georgia*

CLYDE N. WILSON
*Southern Poets and Poems, 1606–1860:
The Land They Loved, Vol. 1*

*Confederate Poets and Poems, Vol. 1
The Land They Loved, Vol. II*

*Confederate Poets and Poems, Vol. 2
The Land They Loved, Vol. III*

Gold–Bug
(Mystery & Suspense Imprint)

BRANDI PERRY
Splintered: A New Orleans Tale

MARTIN WILSON
To Jekyll and Hide